AVOY PUBLISHING
· The Complete Estate & Property Planning Series ·
· Book 3 of 4 ·

PROPERTY AFTER DEATH

What Really Happens to Your Assets

A. Perkins
AVOY PUBLISHING
First Edition · 2026

Property After Death: What Really Happens to Your Assets.

First Edition · 2026 · Printed in the United States of America.

Published in the United States of America by AVOY, LLC ('AVOY Publishing'). AVOY, LLC maintains the worldwide publication and distribution rights to this work.

Permissions and editorial inquiries may be directed to ap@avoyhq.com.

Print ISBN (Hardcover): 978-1-969048-86-9

Print ISBN (Paperback): 978-1-969048-85-2

eBook ISBN: 978-1-969048-87-6

Audiobook ISBN: 978-1-969048-88-3

Cover design and interior typography by AVOY, LLC. Typeset in Georgia and presented in the AVOY house style: burgundy and bronze on cream.

Publisher's Cataloging-in-Publication data available upon request.

For the families who inherit a house

and discover that the deed has its own opinion,

and for the lawyers who explain the difference

between owning a place and living in one.

Estate planning is not paperwork.

It is the form love takes

when it has to outlast

the person who felt it.

Property After Death

LEGAL NOTICE & DISCLAIMER

This book is intended for general educational and informational purposes only. It does not constitute, and is not a substitute for, legal, tax, accounting, investment, real-estate, insurance, or other professional advice. The law of real property, post-mortem title transfer, joint ownership, and trust-held real estate is governed primarily by the individual states; statutes, court rules, recording requirements, judicial decisions, and tax authorities vary materially by jurisdiction and change over time. Application of any concept discussed in these pages to a particular set of facts requires individualized counsel from a qualified, licensed professional admitted to practice in the relevant jurisdiction.

Discussion of state-specific provisions — including the Uniform Probate Code, the Uniform Real Property Transfer on Death Act, the various community-property regimes, and selected statutes of California, Florida, Texas, New York, Nevada, Pennsylvania, Illinois, and other representative jurisdictions — is offered at a conceptual and comparative level. Such discussion is neither exhaustive nor a substitute for the underlying statutes, recording acts, and court rules, which should be consulted directly together with current case law.

Names, fact patterns, and dialogue used in case studies, hypothetical examples, and “What This Looks Like in Practice” sections are illustrative composites. Any resemblance to actual persons, families, decedents, co-owners, trustees, or estates is coincidental and unintentional. No client-lawyer or advisor-client relationship is formed by reading this book or by following any example within it.

References to federal estate, gift, generation-skipping transfer, and income-tax basis rules are grounded in the Internal Revenue Code as in effect at the time of writing. Federal exemption amounts, basis-step-up rules, and procedural requirements change. Readers should obtain current figures and current guidance before acting on any statement in this volume.

Neither the author nor AVOY, LLC, nor any contributor, editor, or reviewer accepts liability for any loss or damage caused, directly or indirectly, by reliance on the contents of this book. Readers are urged to obtain individualized professional advice before recording, transferring, partitioning, selling, refinancing, gifting, or otherwise relying upon any matter of post-mortem property ownership.

By continuing to read this book, the reader acknowledges and accepts the terms of this notice.

CONTENTS

A LETTER FROM THE PUBLISHER

"Estate planning is not paperwork. It is the form love takes when it has to outlast the person who felt it."

If you have opened this book, you are almost certainly one of three kinds of reader.

You may be someone who has just inherited — or believes you have inherited — a house, a piece of land, a vacation property, or a share of one. The deed in your hand carries a name that is no longer alive. You have been told, by a lawyer or by a relative, that the property cannot simply be transferred the way the family expected. There is talk of probate, of joint tenancy, of a trust no one funded properly. You are tired, you are grieving, and the house — which had been a fixed point in the family's life — has become unfamiliar terrain.

You may be someone who is alive and well and trying to plan. You have read that probate is to be avoided. You have heard that putting a child on the deed solves the problem. You suspect, correctly, that the truth is more complicated than that, and you would like — just once — to find a book that tells you what each of these mechanisms actually does, what each one costs, and what each one quietly forecloses.

Or you may be the executor, trustee, or family member who has been asked to figure out, on behalf of others, who the property now belongs to. The answer turns out to depend less on what anyone wanted and more on how the title was held — a sentence of property law that strangers wrote into the deed years ago and that the family has only now been forced to read.

This book is for all three of you.

Property After Death is Book 3 of The Complete Estate & Property Planning Series — a four-volume institutional reference comprising Trust Made Simple (Book 1), Probate Explained (Book 2), Property After Death (Book 3, this volume), and Estate Taxes Explained (Book 4). The series, taken together, treats the four pillars of American post-mortem asset transfer. This volume picks up where Probate Explained leaves off and treats, in detail, the single asset category that produces more confusion, more litigation, and more intrafamily fracture than any other in American estate practice: real property — houses, land, condominiums, vacation homes, family farms, fractional interests, and the recorded paper that controls them all.

The book takes a position. It says that property law is precise, that the deed already contains the answer, and that most disputes after a death are really arguments with a piece of paper that was signed years before anyone knew it would matter. The argument is rarely won. The deed is patient and literal. Once you understand what it actually says, the conflict almost always resolves — sometimes amicably, sometimes not, but always by the rules the document already set.

"Houses do not pass to the people who loved them most. They pass to the people whose names appear on the deed, in the form the deed prescribes. Everything else is a wish."

We have written it on the assumption that you are an intelligent adult who has been talked down to enough times by people in suits. Where the law is technical, we say so. Where it is not, we use ordinary words. Where the outcome depends on a state-by-state distinction — community property, transfer-on-death deeds, the existence or absence of a partition statute, the recording requirements, the homestead protections, the tenancy by the entirety — we point that out and tell you which states fall on which side of the line.

We have also written it on the assumption that you may have a house in your own name, in joint tenancy with a spouse, as a tenant in common with siblings, in a revocable trust, in an LLC, or in some combination of all five — and that what happens at death is sharply different in each of those worlds. We will treat all of them. We will not pretend that one form is universally better than another. The right answer, in property law, is almost always: it depends on the family and on the structure that family actually has.

Particular care has been taken with the moments when families typically stumble: the first call to the title company, the discovery of an outdated joint tenant, the surprise of a co-tenant's intestate share, the trust that was signed but never funded, the ancillary probate in a second state, the occupancy disagreement between the heir who lived there and the heir who did not. Each of those moments has its own logic. Each has its own way of producing avoidable conflict. We will spend time on all of them.

We are not your lawyer. The Legal Notice on the previous page is not ceremonial. Property law sits at the intersection of state recording acts, federal tax basis rules, and the lived realities of families that learn the rules during the hardest week of their lives. A book can show you the architecture. It cannot draft your particular deed. When you act on something in these pages, do it with the help of qualified counsel in the relevant jurisdiction.

With that, we offer you the volume.

— AVOY Publishing

Spring 2026

HOW TO READ THIS BOOK

The book is organized in six movements.

You can read them in order, the way they were written, and you will end up with a complete mental model of how real property moves at and after death: who owned it, what the deed actually said, what transferred automatically, what got pulled into court, why families fought, and how ownership eventually resolved. By the time you reach the Conclusion you will know more about property after death than ninety-five percent of the population — including most adult children and most surviving spouses who arrive at the title company for the first time.

Or you can read whichever Part answers the question you came with. Each chapter stands alone. The cross-references will get you back to anything you skipped.

A few suggestions, depending on who you are.

If you have just inherited — or think you have inherited — a property.
Read Chapter 6 first. It treats the three paths a house can travel after a death: automatic transfer, trust transfer, and probate transfer. Then read Chapter 1 (ownership versus occupancy) and Chapter 2 (why the deed controls). Those three chapters together will tell you, with reasonable confidence, which path your property is on.

If you co-own property with a parent, sibling, or business partner.
Read Chapter 3 (joint tenancy) and Chapter 4 (tenants in common). The two ownership forms look almost identical on the recorded page and behave completely differently at death. Most of the surprise litigation in this field comes from people who were sure they held one form and discovered, afterward, they held the other.

If you have a trust — or have been told you should have one.
Read Chapter 5. A trust that holds title behaves nothing like a trust that exists only on paper. Chapter 5 explains the difference, names the single most common failure (unfunded property), and supplies the questions to ask your estate planner before you assume the work is done.

If you are an executor, trustee, or successor trustee facing a property decision now.

Read Chapter 7 (why houses get pulled into court), Chapter 10 (how ownership resolves), Appendix C (the property checklist), and Appendix G (the post-mortem property timeline). These four sections together cover roughly ninety percent of what your role will require.

A note on the prose. Where the book uses a technical term — joint tenancy, tenancy by the entirety, transfer-on-death deed, ancillary probate, partition, basis step-up — the term is defined the first time it appears, and re-defined any time it shows up in a chapter where the reader may have lost the thread. Where the law is truly complicated, we say so and slow down. Where it is not, we move quickly. The Glossary in the back catches anything that drifts.

A Note on the Reading Conventions

Three small visual conventions appear throughout the book. They are easy to recognize and worth understanding before you begin.

Chapter at a Glance

Every chapter opens with a short bullet list under the heading "Chapter at a Glance." It tells you what the chapter is about and what you will know by the end. Read it as a map. Skip it if you would rather discover the territory as you go.

KEY POINT callouts

Boxed in burgundy with a “KEY POINT” label, these are the most important structural facts in each chapter — the sentences that, if you remembered nothing else from a given chapter, would still leave you better informed than ninety percent of readers approaching the subject for the first time. If you are skim-reading, read the KEY POINT boxes.

REFLECTION callouts

Boxed in bronze with a “REFLECTION” label, these are quieter notes — observations about how the procedure intersects with families, with grief, or with the deeper question of what property law is really protecting. They are not summaries. They are pauses. Skip them if you are reading in a hurry; return to them later when the work is closer.

WHO OWNS THE HOUSE? definition box

Boxed in steel-blue and labeled “WHO OWNS THE HOUSE?”, this single callout appears in the Preface and supplies the working answer to the question that drives the entire book. If you read nothing else before Chapter 1, read that box.

What This Looks Like in Practice

Most chapters include a short narrative vignette under this heading. The vignettes are illustrative composites — names and details are invented, but the patterns they describe are common in property practice. They are intended to ground the abstract architecture of the chapter in the texture of a real family's experience.

Tables, Figures, and the Glossary

Tables are labeled "Table X.X" and figures are labeled "Figure X.X." They are integrated into the text where they help, never as decoration. The Glossary in the back of the book defines every technical term used in the chapters; if a word stops you, the Glossary will start you again.

What's at the Back of This Book

Roughly the back third of this volume is reference material. It is meant to be returned to long after the first reading, when the work is no longer abstract. We list it here so you know what is waiting for you when you need it.

- **Conclusion.** The philosophical close — what property law is for, in plain language.
- **Reader FAQ.** Common questions, organized by category — Ownership & Title, Trusts & Deeds, and Disputes & Resolution — with every answer cross-referenced to the chapter that treats it in full.

- **Glossary of Property-After-Death Terms.** More than forty entries. Every technical word in the book, defined in plain English, with chapter cross-references.
- **Bibliography & Reference Guide.** Statutory sources, treatises, practitioner guides, periodicals, and online resources for the reader who wants to dig deeper.
- **About the Publisher and About the Author.** AVOY Publishing's mission and the author's background.
- **Fourteen Appendices (A–N).** Property at a Glance · Survivorship Forms by State · The Heir's Property Checklist · Common Deed Forms and What They Mean · Sample Property Letter of Instruction · Annotated Reading List · Twelve-Month Property Resolution Calendar · Co-Tenant Communication Framework · Subject Index · Reader's Quick-Start Guide · Notes on The Complete Estate & Property Planning Series · Chapter-by-Chapter Summary · Basis Step-Up Tables · Ancillary Probate and Multi-State Property.

Together the back matter is a compact reference library. If you came to the book in crisis, the Reader's Quick-Start Guide (Appendix J) and the Heir's Property Checklist (Appendix C) will be the most useful pages you read this week.

Begin where it serves you. Return as your circumstances change. The book is designed for both first reading and tenth.

A NOTE ON THE MAKING OF THIS VOLUME

◆

A book like this could be written in two ways.

It could be written by a real-property lawyer, in the language real-property lawyers use, with citations to recording statutes on every page and a chapter on the rule against perpetuities that nobody finishes. Several such books exist. They are useful to lawyers.

Or it could be written by someone who has watched property change hands from the other side of the closing table — who has sat with surviving spouses while the title officer explained why a deed could not yet be recorded, watched siblings negotiate the future of a parents' house without realizing they each owned only a one-third interest, watched trusts that looked airtight on paper unravel because no one had moved the deed, and listened to the same misunderstandings repeat themselves across a hundred different families. That is the perspective from which this book is written.

The author is not a real-property lawyer and does not pretend to be one. He is, however, someone who has spent more than a decade observing private estate administration in close proximity — as an executor, as a trustee, as a co-tenant, as the settlor of trusts that hold title to real property in multiple states, and as the person whom families in his orbit have turned to when they did not know who else to ask. The result is a book that takes property law seriously without pretending to be the law itself.

Where the text describes a state recording statute, a partition rule, or a community-property doctrine, the description is grounded in the rule as it stood at the time of writing. Where the text describes how title actually moves in real life, the description is grounded in observation of how it has moved for real families over the past decade and longer.

This is, in short, a practitioner's book — written for readers who would rather understand the architecture than be sold a brochure of it.

PREFACE

The first thing to know about real property after death is that the deed is older, calmer, and more literal than anyone in the family.

It does not care who lived in the house. It does not care who paid the mortgage. It does not care who slept in the back bedroom for twenty years and who never visited. It cares only what it says — the names printed on the recorded page, the form of ownership those names share, and the conditions, if any, that the document expressly attaches to the transfer.

> **WHO OWNS THE HOUSE?**
>
> WHO OWNS THE HOUSE? At any moment in time, the legal owner of a parcel of real property is whoever appears on the most recently recorded valid deed, in the form of ownership that deed prescribes, subject only to operation of law (death of a joint tenant) or further recorded instrument. Occupancy, sentiment, and family history do not move title. Only paper does.

Property law in the United States has spent centuries refining this principle. The recording acts of every state — some descended from the English Statute of Enrolments of 1535, some written from scratch in the nineteenth century — exist precisely so that a stranger can walk into a county recorder's office and answer the question "who owns this?" without consulting the family. The deed is a public, datable, machine-readable, jurisdiction-bound document. It exists so the family is not the source of authority on its own property.

When a property owner dies, the deed does not change. The owner is gone; the recorded ownership is not. What happens next depends on what the deed actually said — the form of co-ownership, if any; the presence of a survivorship clause, if any; the existence of a transfer-on-death designation, if any; whether title was held in the name of an individual, a couple, a trust, or an entity. Each of those choices, made years before the death, controls almost everything that happens after it.

Real property is the asset American families most often own and most often misunderstand. It is the largest single line item on most household balance sheets. It is the asset most charged with memory. It is the asset most likely to outlast its owner by decades. And it is the asset whose post-mortem path is the most precisely choreographed by the deed.

We will move through it in stages. We will begin with the structural distinction between ownership and occupancy, because almost every subsequent problem in this field begins with their conflation. We will move into the deed itself — why it controls, why a will cannot override it for property whose deed already prescribes a transfer, and why two people with identical wills can produce sharply different outcomes. We will spend the middle of the book on the three forms of co-ownership that account for nearly all American real-property holdings — joint tenancy with right of survivorship, tenancy in common, and trust-titled property — and on the three paths a house can travel after a death. We will turn in Part V to the human side: why families fight over houses, what those fights are really about, and what tools exist to defuse them. We will close in Part VI with the question of how property ownership finally resolves — cleanly when the title is clear, slowly when it is not.

Read with patience. The subject rewards it.

INTRODUCTION

Why This Book Exists

◆

When someone dies, money matters.

But the house matters more.

It is usually the largest asset. It carries emotional weight. It is where people lived, gathered, argued, celebrated, and remember. And it is also the asset families misunderstand the most.

Confusion about property ownership after death causes more conflict, delay, and resentment than almost anything else in estate administration — not because people are unreasonable, but because property law is rarely explained clearly. Most adults learn the rules for the first time at a closing table, in the office of a title officer, while a family member is still being remembered.

This book exists to answer one question, and to answer it honestly:

Who actually owns the property now?

Once that question is answered, most disputes resolve themselves. The remaining ones become tractable. The path forward stops being a matter of negotiation and becomes a matter of execution.

Property after death feels intrusive, slow, and intimidating not because the law is cruel, but because ownership is precise. The deed was written in a moment when no one expected it would matter the way it now does. The form of ownership chosen — sometimes deliberately, more often by default at a closing thirty years ago — controls every subsequent question. The mismatch between the family's expectations and the deed's literal terms is the source of nearly every post-mortem property dispute on record.

This book exists for one reason: to explain how real property actually moves at and after death — without fear, without salesmanship, and without pretending the answer is simpler than it is.

Real property does not pass to the people who loved the house most.

It does not pass to the family member who lived there the longest.

It does not pass to the heir who paid the property taxes for the last decade.

It passes — in every American jurisdiction, every time — to the person or persons identified by the deed, in the form of ownership the deed prescribes, subject only to operation of law and to the further recorded instruments that have come after.

Once you understand that single principle, the rest of the architecture becomes legible.

Every year, a very large number of American families lose meaningful value, time, and family cohesion to four things they could have anticipated and did not.

The first is mistaken survivorship — the family member who believed a joint deed conveyed survivorship rights and discovers, on the recording page, that it conveyed only a tenancy in common, with the deceased's share now passing through probate to whoever happens to inherit it.

The second is unfunded trusts — the carefully drafted plan that named every beneficiary, vested every power, and was signed in front of witnesses, but that nobody ever bothered to retitle the house into. The trust exists. The deed still names the deceased individually. The house goes through probate.

The third is multi-state real property — the second home in another state, the inherited farmland three states away, the time-share condominium across the river. Each property recorded in a foreign jurisdiction usually requires its own ancillary probate. A single asset in a different state can double the time and cost of administration.

The fourth is co-tenant disagreement — the siblings, cousins, or blended-family members who collectively inherit fractional interests in a single property and discover they cannot agree on what to do with it. The law does not require them to agree. It supplies, in every state, a remedy of last resort: a partition action, conducted in court, that ends the co-tenancy by sale or by physical division. It is the most painful proceeding in the field.

Each of these four costs can be planned for. Some can be avoided entirely with the right titling chosen during life. Most can be sharply reduced even after the structure is already set, if the family engages the question early.

This book exists because most of what is written about property after death is written either for lawyers — and is therefore unreadable to anyone else — or for marketing purposes, and is therefore not telling the whole truth. The space in the middle — a book that respects the reader's intelligence, defines its terms, takes the law seriously, names what each ownership form can and cannot do, and tells the truth about the practical experience of inheriting a piece of real estate — has been mostly empty.

We wrote this volume to fill it.

By the time you finish, you will know:

- What ownership of real property is, structurally — and why it is not the same as occupancy.
- Why the deed controls and the will is, for many properties, irrelevant to disposition.

- What joint tenancy with right of survivorship is, what it does, and what it quietly forecloses.
- What tenancy in common is, why it is the default in many states, and why it produces fractional probate.
- What it actually means for a property to be "owned by a trust," and how to tell whether yours really is.
- The three paths a house can travel after a death — and how to recognize which path applies to yours.
- Why even thoughtful estate plans get pulled into court — and the small handful of structural failures that account for most cases.
- What common property disputes after death are really about, and which of them the law can solve.
- Why families fight over houses with such intensity — and what defuses the conflict before it escalates.
- How property ownership finally resolves, and what life looks like once it has.

This is not legal advice. It is a foundation. With it, you will be in a position to ask better questions, evaluate better answers, and make better decisions about a process that arrives, sooner or later, in nearly every American family that has ever owned a piece of real estate.

That is the value of a book like this.

Let us begin.

PART I

◆

FOUNDATIONS

Why ownership is precise, why the deed controls, and why occupancy is not the same as title.

CHAPTER 1

Ownership Is Not the Same as Occupancy

Chapter at a Glance

- Why occupancy and ownership are different categories — and why almost every post-mortem property surprise begins with their conflation.
- What the deed actually does, and why the recording act exists in the form it does.
- Three particularly common misconceptions: constructive ownership through possession, moral ownership through caregiving, and survivorship through cohabitation.
- What questions the law asks after death — and what questions it does not.
- How to read Table 1.1 — what each ownership status gives you and what it does not.

Many families assume that the person living in the house owns the house. That assumption is often wrong.

Ownership is not about who lives there, who pays the bills, or who maintains the property. Ownership is about how title is held — the form of words on the most recently recorded deed, the names listed in those words, and the relationship the law assigns to those names.

It is one of the more durable confusions in American family life. The adult child who has lived in the parents' house for twenty years, paid the property taxes, replaced the roof, and cared for the parents in their final illness has not, by virtue of any of those acts, acquired ownership of the house. The widow who has occupied the marital home for forty years but whose name was never added to the deed does not, for that reason alone, own the home. The cousin who inherited a one-eighth interest in the family farm thirty years ago, has never set foot on the property, and could not point to it on a map, owns exactly that one-eighth interest — no less and no more.

These outcomes feel unfair when they appear, but they are not accidents. They are the operation of a system that was built, deliberately, to separate possession from ownership. The separation is the entire point of the recording act.

What the Deed Does

A deed is not a receipt. It is not a memorial. It is not a description of who lives where or who paid for what. A deed is a legal instrument that conveys an interest in real property from one person (the grantor) to another (the grantee). When properly executed and recorded, it is the document the law treats as definitive on the question of who owns the land.

Every parcel of real property in the United States has a recorded title history — a chain of deeds running from the original sovereign grant down to the present owner — and the deed at the top of that chain is the deed that controls. A grantor cannot convey what the grantor does not own. A grantee takes only what the deed describes. The recording acts of every state ensure that this chain is publicly searchable so that buyers, lenders, heirs, creditors, and courts can answer the ownership question without consulting the family.

> **KEY POINT**
>
> Ownership of real property is determined by the most recently recorded valid deed, in the form of ownership that deed prescribes. Occupancy, financial contribution, family expectation, and personal sacrifice are not factors the recording act considers. Only the paper does.

Three Familiar Misconceptions

Three particular misconceptions about ownership account for most of the confusion families experience after a death. They are worth naming directly, because each of them has consequences that the family will eventually meet.

(1) The misconception of constructive ownership through possession. The adult child who has lived in the parents' home for two decades, paid every utility bill, and maintained the property assumes that the law will recognize this contribution and treat the home as theirs. It will not. There exists a doctrine called adverse possession that, in narrow circumstances, can

ripen long-term occupancy into title — but it requires occupancy that is hostile to the record owner's interest, and the family member who lives in the parents' house with the parents' permission satisfies none of its elements. Permission is the opposite of hostility. The doctrine exists for the squatter and the trespasser, not the dutiful child.

(2) The misconception of moral ownership through caregiving. The family member who provided years of unpaid care to a parent often feels — reasonably — that the law should recognize this contribution. It generally does not. There are statutory schemes (Medicaid caregiver-child exceptions, sweat-equity claims in some states, promises that ripen into enforceable contracts under particular factual showings) that occasionally provide relief. They are the exception. The default rule is that gratuitous services are gratuitous — gifts to the family, not consideration for an unwritten transfer of real property.

(3) The misconception of survivorship through cohabitation. The long-term unmarried partner who has shared a home for many years but whose name was never added to the deed has, on the death of the owner, no automatic ownership interest at all. Some jurisdictions recognize palimony or constructive-trust theories that may produce relief under specific facts; most do not, and even where the theories exist they are slow, expensive, and uncertain. The cleanest path is always to put the partner on

the deed during life — a five-minute drafting decision that prevents years of subsequent litigation.

Why the Law Works This Way

It is worth pausing to ask why the system separates ownership from occupancy. The reasons are old and durable.

Real property is, by its nature, immobile and durable. It outlasts its owners by decades and sometimes centuries. The same parcel may have a hundred different owners over the course of its history. For the system to work — for buyers, lenders, creditors, and inheritors to have any confidence in the chain of title — there must be a publicly searchable record that does not depend on who happens to be living on the land at any given moment.

If the law treated occupancy as evidence of ownership, every purchaser would have to interview the neighbors, every lender would have to verify the residents, and every estate would face decades of potential claims from anyone who had ever stayed in the house. The system would be unworkable. The recording act exists to make the system work — and the price of making it work is that occupancy and ownership are kept rigorously distinct.

What the Law Asks After Death

After a death, the law does not ask:

- Who needs the house?

- Who lived there longest?
- Who paid the mortgage?
- Who took care of the parent?
- Who deserves to inherit it?

It asks:

- Who holds legal title?
- What form of co-ownership, if any, is on the deed?
- What does the deed direct upon the death of the named owner?

These three questions, in this order, determine what happens next. Every other question — emotional, moral, practical — is downstream of them. Understanding this ordering eliminates most of the confusion that surrounds property after death.

Table 1.1

Status	Right to live there	Right to sell	Inherits at death
Sole owner of record	Yes	Yes	Per deed, will, or intestate law
Joint tenant with right of survivorship	Yes	Joint signature required	Survivor takes by operation of law
Tenant in common	Yes	Joint signature; partition available	Decedent's share passes through estate
Beneficiary of a funded trust	Per trust terms	Trustee acts	Per trust terms
Long-term occupant, no deed interest	Only with owner's consent	No	No automatic right
Surviving spouse, not on deed	Per state homestead/elective share	No (without title)	Per state spousal protections; otherwise none
Caregiver, not on deed	Only with owner's consent	No	No automatic right
Tenant under lease	Per lease term	No	Lease may survive owner death

Occupancy versus ownership — what each gives you, and what it does not.

Table 1.1 makes the structural point clearly. Occupancy and ownership are different categories. Each has its own bundle of rights. Each produces its own outcome at death. Confusing one for the other is the single most common source of post-mortem property surprise.

What This Looks Like in Practice — A Brief Preview

The chapters that follow will return to these distinctions repeatedly. Chapter 2 will explain why the deed controls and the will, for many properties, does not. Chapter 3 will address joint tenancy — the ownership form that produces automatic transfer at death — and Chapter 4 will treat tenancy in common, which does not. Chapter 5 will treat trust-held property. Chapter 6 will assemble these mechanisms into the three paths a house can travel after a death.

But none of those mechanisms will be coherent if the reader is still carrying the assumption that the family member living in the house is the person who owns it. That assumption is the first thing to set down. Everything in this book follows from setting it down.

Where We Go From Here

What This Looks Like in Practice

Consider a family — call them the Reyes family. The mother, Maria, died at age eighty-one after a long illness. Her younger son, Esteban, had moved into Maria's home eight years earlier to care for her after her stroke. He paid the property taxes, replaced the roof in the third year, and handled every domestic decision the household made from the day he arrived.

Esteban's older sister, Rosa, lived three states away. She visited annually and sent monthly cards. She had not contributed financially to the household but had remained in regular contact with Maria throughout.

Maria's will, drafted in 2009 from a kit, left her estate equally to her two children. Maria had told Esteban, on multiple occasions, that he should keep the house — his work as her caregiver, in her view, more than balanced any inequality. She did not, however, retitle the deed. She did not sign a transfer-on-death deed. She did not amend her will.

When Maria died, Esteban learned what his eight years of occupancy and contribution had legally produced: nothing. The house was titled in Maria's individual name. Maria's will controlled. The will divided the estate equally. Rosa was entitled to half. Esteban could buy out Rosa's interest, sell the house and split the proceeds, or petition for partition. He could not simply keep living there as the owner; he was the owner of half, and Rosa was the owner of the other half.

The story is not unusual. The cure — a transfer-on-death deed signed during life, or a single retitling deed into joint tenancy with Esteban — would have cost a few hundred dollars and would have settled the question permanently. The cure was not implemented. The result is the system's default, applied to a family whose history and contributions the deed could not see.

The remainder of Part I lays the foundation. Chapter 2 takes up the deed itself — what it does, why it controls, and why two people with identical wills can produce sharply different outcomes. Part II moves into the three principal forms of co-ownership: joint tenancy (Chapter 3) and tenancy in common (Chapter 4). Part III treats trust-held property (Chapter 5). Parts IV through VI take up what happens at death (Chapters 6 and 7), why families fight (Chapters 8 and 9), and how ownership finally resolves (Chapter 10).

Notes on Practice

Two practical patterns are worth flagging here, before the next chapter takes up the deed itself. First, the family member who has lived in a parents' home for many years often carries an emotional ledger that the legal system does not recognize: years of caregiving, decades of property maintenance, sacrifices made in income or career to be physically present. The deed records none of this. The legal outcome and the emotional accounting are separate ledgers. Where the parents wish to recognize the contribution, the place to do it is on the deed during life — not in a precatory letter the family will read for the first time at the funeral.

Second, the long-term unmarried partner is one of the most underprotected categories in American property law. The partner who has shared a home for decades but whose name was never added to the deed has, on the death of the owner, essentially no automatic protection in most jurisdictions. The cure — adding the partner to the deed during life as a joint tenant or co-trustee, or recording a transfer-on-death deed in the partner's favor — is straightforward. The alternative is the kind of subsequent litigation that frequently fails on its merits and always damages the surviving partner's grief.

Common Questions, Briefly

If I lived in the house and paid all the expenses, can the court grant me ownership?

Generally no, unless you can establish one of three narrow doctrines. The first is adverse possession, which requires occupancy that is open, notorious, exclusive, continuous, and hostile to the record owner's interest for the statutory period (commonly five to twenty years, depending on state). Adverse possession does not run against an owner who has given you permission to occupy — and family members occupying with implicit family consent satisfy none of its elements. The second is constructive trust, which requires evidence that the record owner held title for your benefit under an oral or implied agreement. Constructive-trust claims are evidentiary burdens with low success rates. The third is equitable lien, which can recover the value of contributions you made to the property under specific facts. Equitable liens are partial remedies — they recover money, not ownership.

Can my parent's verbal promise that the house would be mine override the deed?

Almost never. Real-property transfers must be in writing under the Statute of Frauds, an English-law inheritance that every American state has codified in some form. A few jurisdictions recognize an exception called partial performance — where the promisee has substantially performed actions consistent with ownership (paid the mortgage for years, made significant improvements, treated the property as theirs to the parent's knowledge) — but the exception is narrow and difficult to establish. The cleanest cure is a written instrument signed by the owner during life: a deed, a transfer-on-death designation, or a will that specifically addresses the property.

A Closer Look at the Recording Act

The recording act is one of the oldest mechanisms in American private law, and its operation deserves a moment of close attention. Every state has one. The function is the same everywhere: to provide constructive notice to the world of every recorded interest in real property, so that buyers, lenders, creditors, and inheritors can rely on the public record without needing to investigate every prior transaction individually.

The recording acts come in three doctrinal flavors. A race-notice statute (the most common) protects a subsequent purchaser who records first AND who took without notice of the prior unrecorded interest. A pure-notice statute protects any subsequent purchaser without notice, regardless of recording order. A pure-race statute protects whoever records first, regardless of notice. The differences matter in title litigation but rarely in family inheritance, where all interests are usually recorded.

What the recording act does NOT do is investigate the substance of recorded instruments. The recorder accepts deeds for filing. The recorder does not adjudicate whether the grantor had capacity, whether the deed was procured by undue influence, whether the legal description matches what the parties intended, or whether the named grantee actually exists. Those questions are for the courts. The recording office is a filing system, not a validating one. This distinction explains why a recorded deed can later be set aside by a court — the recording is presumptive evidence of the transfer, not conclusive proof of its validity.

For inheriting families, the practical consequence is that every recorded instrument in the chain is a starting point for analysis, not the end of one. A title-company search will reveal what is recorded. It will not reveal what should not have been recorded. Where the recorded chain is unclear or where there is reason to suspect a defect (a deed signed by a person of doubtful capacity, a deed in which the grantor's signature looks suspect, a deed that conveys an interest the grantor did not have), counsel should be engaged to evaluate the substance behind the record.

The cost is modest. The subsequent litigation, if avoided, can be substantial.

Practitioner Patterns — Beyond the Categories

Three additional patterns surface frequently in real-property estates that deserve a closer look before we move on. Each involves the same conflation of occupancy and ownership treated above, but in fact patterns the reader is likely to encounter personally or in immediate family.

The first is what practitioners call the silent-deed scenario: the family member who has been told, repeatedly and convincingly, that they will inherit a particular property — and who has organized their life around that expectation — but for whom no actual instrument was ever signed. The promise may have been earnest. The intent may have been real. The problem is that intent without paper is not ownership. When the property owner dies, the silent deed produces nothing. The inheritor's only recourse is the narrow constructive-trust theory described above, which succeeds in only a small minority of contested cases. The lesson is uncomfortable but durable: every promise about real property should be reduced to a recorded instrument during the promisor's lifetime, even when the family relationship makes the formality feel cold.

The second is the elderly-parent-and-helpful-neighbor scenario. An elderly parent, increasingly isolated, develops a friendship with a neighbor who provides daily assistance —

grocery runs, medication management, transportation to medical appointments. Over time, the parent comes to refer to the neighbor as family. After the parent's death, the neighbor sometimes asserts a claim to the property based on alleged promises, alleged contributions, or alleged constructive trust. The claim may have substance; it may not. The litigation that follows is uniformly painful for the actual heirs, who often did not know about the neighbor's involvement until it was too late to address. The cure during life is regular family visits and documented family communication — not because the neighbor is necessarily acting in bad faith, but because the absence of family contact creates a vacuum that subsequent claimants can fill.

The third is the multi-decade family-property scenario. A property has been in the family for three or four generations. Various family members have lived in it at various times. Over the decades, several deeds have been recorded, several intestate successions have occurred, and several family members have made improvements without formal documentation of who paid for what. By the time the current generation is ready to sell or refinance, the title chain is a thicket of partial interests, undocumented transfers, and contested contributions. Title-chain reconstruction (treated in Chapter 7) is the cure, but it can take months and several thousand dollars. The lesson here is that intergenerational property deserves intergenerational attention: every generation that lives with the property should clean up the chain on its watch, not leave it for the next.

The book is long because the subject is layered. Read the parts you need.

> **KEY POINT**
>
> Real-property ownership is determined by the most recently recorded valid deed, in the form of ownership that deed prescribes. Occupancy, financial contribution, and family expectation are not factors the recording act considers.

What This Chapter Has Said

Ownership is not the same as occupancy. The family member who lives in the parents' house, the caregiver who provided years of unpaid service, the long-term unmarried partner whose name was never added to the deed — none of these statuses, by themselves, conveys ownership. The recording act exists specifically to separate possession from title, and three centuries of American property practice have reinforced that separation. Most post-mortem property surprises trace, at their root, to the conflation of the two categories. Setting the conflation down — accepting that occupancy and ownership answer different questions — is the first work of any honest post-mortem property analysis.

CHAPTER 2

Why Deeds Matter More Than Wills

Chapter at a Glance

- Why a deed transfers property and a will only expresses intent.
- The five principal forms of real-property ownership for natural persons, and how each behaves at death.
- Why two people can sign identical wills and produce sharply different outcomes — because their deeds are different.
- When the deed and the will disagree, why the deed prevails for any transfer the deed already prescribes.
- What the will does add — appointment of the executor, control of unfunded property, and precatory direction for property already disposed of.

A will does not transfer property. A deed does.

This surprises many people. They have heard their entire adult lives that the will is the document — the master instruction set, the controlling statement of who gets what. They are right about a great many assets. They are wrong, in a particular and important way, about real property whose deed already prescribes its own transfer.

A will expresses intent. A deed establishes ownership.

If a property is titled in a way that transfers automatically at death — joint tenancy with right of survivorship, tenancy by the entirety, transfer-on-death deed, Lady-Bird deed, or trust ownership — the will is irrelevant to that property. The deed has already spoken. The will has nothing to add.

If a property is titled in a way that requires court involvement — an individually owned asset with no transfer-on-death mechanism, a tenancy-in-common interest with no survivorship feature — the will directs disposition of that interest, but only after a probate court has confirmed the will and authorized the transfer. The deed still controls the form; the will controls the destination.

This is why two people can leave identical wills and produce very different outcomes. The will is the same. The deeds are not. The deeds — drafted years before, in moments nobody remembers — control first. The will applies only to what the deed allows to be willed.

What a Deed Actually Says

The body of a deed contains, at minimum, four things: the names of the grantors (the persons conveying); the names of the grantees (the persons receiving); the legal description of the property; and the form of ownership the grantees take. Most deeds also recite consideration, contain warranty or quitclaim language, and identify any encumbrances (mortgages, easements, restrictions). The form-of-ownership language is the part that controls what happens at death.

Compare two phrases that look almost identical:

- "To John Smith and Mary Smith, husband and wife, as joint tenants with right of survivorship."
- "To John Smith and Mary Smith, husband and wife, as tenants in common."

Both phrases convey title to the same two people, in the same marriage, who will live in the same house. The first creates automatic transfer at death — when John dies, Mary becomes sole owner without any court involvement at all. The second does not. Under the second, when John dies, Mary owns her one-half interest and John's half passes through John's estate, by will or by intestate succession, to whoever is entitled to it. If John's will leaves everything to Mary, Mary eventually receives the second half — but only after probate. If John has no will, John's half passes by state intestate succession, which in many states gives some share to the children rather than the surviving spouse.

The same words, the same people, the same house. Two completely different post-death stories. The difference is six words on the deed.

KEY POINT

The form of ownership recited on the deed controls the transfer at death. The will controls disposition only of property that has not already been disposed of by the deed itself. Where the deed and the will appear to disagree, the deed prevails for any transfer the deed already prescribes.

The Five Principal Forms of Real-Property Ownership

American real-property law recognizes five principal forms of ownership for natural persons. Each behaves differently at death. Recognizing which form applies to a given parcel is the first work of any post-mortem property analysis.

Table 2.1

Form	Lifetime control	Behavior at death
Sole ownership (one named owner)	Owner has full control	Passes through probate per will or intestate law.
Joint tenancy with right of survivorship	Either co-owner can sever by transfer	Survivor takes automatically by operation of law.
Tenancy by the entirety (married couples; some states)	Neither spouse can sever unilaterally	Survivor takes automatically; creditor protection during life.
Tenancy in common	Each co-owner controls own share independently	Decedent's share passes through estate.
Trust ownership (revocable or irrevocable)	Trustee controls per trust terms	Successor trustee continues administration outside probate.

The five principal forms of real-property ownership and their behavior at death.

Beyond these five, real property may also be held by entities (LLCs, partnerships, corporations) and by life-estate arrangements (in which the holder owns the property for life and a remainderman takes at death). These are less common in residential settings and are treated as variants in Chapter 5 and Appendix N. The five forms above account for the great majority of American residential and small-investment real estate.

When the Deed and the Will Disagree

It is common for a family, after a death, to discover that the deceased's will and the recorded deed point in different directions. The will leaves the marital home to the surviving spouse. The deed shows the home held in joint tenancy with the deceased's adult son from a prior marriage. Or the will leaves the family farm equally to three children. The deed shows the farm held as tenants in common with one of the three children already named — meaning that child owns half the farm outright and the deceased's half passes through the will, producing a final distribution of one-half plus one-sixth to the named co-owner and one-sixth to each of the others.

In every case, the deed prevails for any transfer the deed itself prescribes. The will operates only on what is left.

This is not an injustice. It is the system functioning. The deed was recorded; the recording act gave it priority; subsequent purchasers, lenders, and creditors relied on it. A will, drafted later, cannot retroactively undo what the deed already did. The order of operations is fixed: deed first, will second.

Why Identical Wills Produce Different Outcomes

Two siblings — call them Anna and Bea — have a parent who dies. The parent left, in each case, a will of about a page and a half, drafted from a kit, leaving everything equally to the deceased's three children. The wills are nearly identical. The estates are not.

Anna's parent had retitled the family home, twelve years before, into joint tenancy with right of survivorship with Anna alone — intending, the parent had told the family at the time, "to make things easier." At death, the home transfers automatically to Anna. The parent's will, leaving everything equally to the three children, operates only on the parent's bank account, brokerage account, and personal property. Anna receives the entire house. Anna's siblings receive one-third of the bank account, the brokerage account, and the personal property — substantially less than Anna, by an order of magnitude.

Bea's parent did not retitle anything. The same home is still in the parent's name alone. At death, the home passes through probate per the will, equally to the three children. Each child receives a one-third interest in the home, plus a one-third interest in the bank account, the brokerage, and the personal property.

Same will. Same intent (presumably). Same family. Sharply different outcomes. The variable is not the will. The variable is the deed.

Cases like Anna's are extremely common. They produce — in many families — significant intra-sibling conflict, which is treated at length in Chapter 9. The fairness question is genuinely difficult. Did the parent intend, by the joint titling, to favor Anna? Or was the joint titling a convenience, with the parent assuming the will would still control? The deed cannot answer this question. The deed answers only what the deed says. Family negotiation, mediation, litigation, or quiet acceptance — these are the available paths forward, and they are paths through grief, not through paper.

> **REFLECTION**
>
> Most disputes over post-mortem property are not really disputes about who should have inherited the house. They are disputes about whether the deceased understood, when they signed the deed, what the deed would later do. The deed is patient and literal. The family is rarely in a position to challenge it.

What the Will Does Add

We have spent this chapter on what the will does not control. It is worth ending on what it does.

The will controls the disposition of any property that the deed has not already disposed of — sole-owned property, tenancy-in-common interests, property in the deceased's name that escaped a trust funding plan, and property held by an entity in which the deceased held the controlling interest. For these assets, the will is decisive.

The will also controls the appointment of the executor, who will stand in the deceased's shoes for the duration of the administration and who will eventually deliver legal title to the beneficiaries that the will names. Without a will, the court appoints an administrator by statutory priority — typically the spouse, then the children — who performs the same function under intestate-succession law.

The will, finally, can include precatory directions about the deceased's wishes for properties that the deed already disposes of. These directions have no binding force — the deed prevails — but they sometimes influence the recipient. A surviving joint tenant who reads, in the deceased's will, a clearly expressed wish that the house ultimately go to a particular grandchild may carry that wish forward voluntarily. The wish is not enforceable. The honoring of it is the survivor's choice.

The Practical Conclusion

The practical conclusion of this chapter is the same as its opening sentence. A will does not transfer property. A deed does.

What This Looks Like in Practice

Two friends — call them Anna and Bea — each lose a parent in the same calendar year. Both parents owned a single-family home valued at approximately $700,000. Both parents had a will leaving their estate equally to their two children. The wills, in fact, were drafted by the same online template service and contain near-identical language.

Anna's parent had retitled the family home, twelve years before, into joint tenancy with right of survivorship with Anna alone. The retitling was done at the suggestion of a financial advisor who explained it as a way to avoid probate. Nobody discussed how it would interact with the will.

Bea's parent took no titling action. The house remained in the parent's individual name throughout.

Anna's outcome: the house transferred automatically to her at death. The will, leaving everything equally to Anna and her sister, had no effect on the house. Anna received the entire $700,000 of house value, plus her half of the parent's bank account, brokerage, and personal property. Anna's sister received only her half of the bank account, brokerage, and personal property — roughly $90,000 in total.

Bea's outcome: the house went through probate. Bea and her sister inherited it as tenants in common, equally. After eleven months of probate administration and $22,000 in fees, Bea and her sister jointly owned a $700,000 house and equal shares of the rest of the estate. They later sold the house and split the proceeds. Bea netted approximately $340,000.

Same will, sharply different outcomes, all because of a deed signed twelve years before either parent died. The lesson is not that one outcome is right and the other wrong; it is that the deed controls and the will follows — and that families intending equal treatment must align the deeds with the wills, not assume the wills will do the work alone.

Anyone who wishes to control how a piece of real property passes at death must look first at the deed and only second at the will. The deed is the document that needs to match the intent. The will, in the case of real property, is at most a backup plan.

Notes on Practice

Several practical patterns recur in the deed-versus-will interaction. The most common is the family that drafts (or amends) a will to leave property in a particular way without consulting whether the deed will allow that disposition. Where the deed already prescribes a transfer (joint tenancy, TBE, TOD, trust), the will's contrary direction has no effect — but the family does not know this until the post-mortem reveal. Counsel asked to draft a will should, in every case, also review the deeds for every parcel of real property the testator owns. The five minutes of additional work prevents most of the post-mortem surprises in this area.

A second common pattern is the testator who attempts to use a will to disinherit a joint tenant or trust beneficiary. The attempt fails for the reasons set out in this chapter. Where the testator's true wish is to redirect the property, the deed must be revised — usually by recording a new deed during life that severs the joint tenancy, removes the co-owner, or removes the property from the trust. The will alone cannot do this work.

Edge Case — The After-Acquired Property Clause

Most modern wills contain a residuary clause directing all property not specifically devised to a named residuary beneficiary. The residuary clause is a powerful catchall: it captures every asset the testator owned at death that the will did not specifically address. For real property whose deed is silent on disposition (sole ownership, tenancy in common), the residuary clause is what controls.

An after-acquired property clause is a related but narrower device — language saying that the residuary includes property the testator acquires after the will is signed. Most modern residuary clauses include this construction implicitly, but older wills sometimes did not, and a small minority of jurisdictions still require explicit language to capture after-acquired real property in the residuary. Counsel drafting wills for clients with active real-estate acquisition patterns (investors, second-home owners) should confirm the residuary language captures future acquisitions without further amendment.

Edge Case — The Deed Signed Without Capacity

A deed signed by a grantor who lacked legal capacity at the moment of execution is voidable. Lack of capacity in the real-property context typically means the grantor did not understand the nature and effect of the transaction at the time of signing — a standard borrowed from contract law and applied to real-property conveyances by case law in most jurisdictions.

The capacity question arises most often in late-life transfers between elderly parents and adult children: the parent, suffering from dementia or cognitive decline, signs a deed transferring the family home to one child, often with circumstances suggestive of undue influence (the child drafted the deed, the child arranged the notarization, the child was the only person present at signing). After the parent's death, the other children may petition the court to set aside the deed on capacity or undue-influence grounds. These cases are evidentiary, slow, and emotionally costly. The single best prevention is independent counsel for the grantor and a contemporaneous medical opinion supporting capacity for any late-life real-property transfer that departs from the family's prior expectations.

Common Questions, Briefly

If my parent's will leaves the house to me but the deed says joint tenancy with my sibling, what controls?

The deed controls. Your sibling, as the surviving joint tenant, takes the entire house automatically at your parent's death. The will's contrary direction has no effect. Your only remedies are: (a) a will-contest theory based on undue influence in the prior joint-titling decision, (b) a constructive-trust theory based on evidence that your sibling promised to honor the will's direction, or (c) negotiation. All three are difficult; (c) is by far the most common path forward.

Can a deed contradict itself, naming both joint tenancy and tenancy in common?

Yes — and the result is a litigated mess. Deeds with internally inconsistent ownership recitals occasionally appear when do-it-yourself drafting tools are used or when an old deed form was not updated for the parties' actual situation. Courts typically apply the rule of construction that ambiguities are resolved against survivorship (because tenancy in common is the default), but the analysis is fact-specific and the litigation is rarely cheap. The cure is a corrective deed signed by all original grantors and grantees, recorded promptly, that resolves the ambiguity in the parties' actual intent.

Practitioner Patterns — Where the Will Still Matters

Although this chapter has emphasized that the deed controls for property whose form of ownership prescribes a transfer, the will is not irrelevant. It is decisive in five categories that warrant explicit treatment, because families often underestimate how much disposition the will still controls.

First, the will controls all property held in the deceased's individual name without a transfer-on-death overlay. For most American homeowners, this is the great majority of their estate by value — bank accounts in their sole name, brokerage accounts without TOD designations, vehicles, personal effects, and any real property held individually. The will's residuary clause typically captures all of these and directs them to the residuary beneficiary.

Second, the will controls every tenancy-in-common interest the deceased held. As Chapter 4 explains, the deceased's fractional share in TIC property goes through the estate and is directed by the will (or by intestate succession). Families with significant TIC holdings — investors, blended families, heirs-property holders — should give careful thought to how the will addresses those fractional interests, because the will is the only mechanism that controls.

Third, the will controls disposition of any after-acquired property the deceased did not transfer to a non-probate structure during life. The vacation property bought in the last few years and never moved into the trust. The inherited interest received from a parent or sibling and not yet retitled. The default ownership at death is the deceased's individual name, and the will's residuary controls.

Fourth, the will controls the appointment of the executor or personal representative — the one person who has authority to act for the estate and to record any deeds needed to clear title or distribute property. Without a will, this person is appointed by the court using statutory priority. With a will, the deceased chose.

Fifth, the will can include precatory direction (non-binding wishes) about non-probate property. The directions have no legal force — the deed has already spoken — but they can carry moral weight with the recipient. A surviving joint tenant who reads the deceased's clearly expressed wish about the property's eventual destination sometimes honors that wish voluntarily, and the family is better for it.

The remaining chapters of Part II treat the two ownership forms that most commonly produce surprise: joint tenancy (Chapter 3) and tenancy in common (Chapter 4). Both look like ordinary co-ownership on the recorded page. Their behavior at death could not be more different.

Figure 2.1

DEED PRESCRIBES
Will is irrelevant

- Joint tenancy w/ survivorship
- Tenancy by the entirety
- Community property w/ ROS
- Transfer-on-death deed
- Lady-Bird (enhanced life estate)
- Property in revocable trust

DEED IS SILENT
Will controls (after probate)

- Sole ownership
- Tenancy in common
- Trust property never funded
- After-acquired property
- Inherited TIC interest
- Property in stale joint tenancy

Two universes of property at death — what the deed already prescribes versus what the will controls.

KEY POINT

A deed transfers property; a will only expresses intent. For property whose deed prescribes a transfer, the will is irrelevant. The will controls only what the deed leaves to it.

What This Chapter Has Said

Five forms of real-property ownership cover most American residential and small-investment real estate: sole ownership, joint tenancy with right of survivorship, tenancy by the entirety, tenancy in common, and trust ownership. Each behaves differently at death. Where the deed prescribes a transfer (joint tenancy, TBE, TOD, trust), that transfer happens regardless of what the will says. Where the deed does not (sole ownership, tenancy in common), the will controls — but only after probate. Two people with identical wills can produce sharply different outcomes because their deeds were not the same. Anyone who wishes to control how a property passes at death must look first at the deed and only second at the will.

PART II

◆

THE OWNERSHIP MECHANISMS

Joint tenancy, tenancy in common, and the survivorship features that determine what transfers automatically and what does not.

CHAPTER 3

Joint Tenancy and the Myth of "It Just Goes to Them"

Chapter at a Glance

- What joint tenancy with right of survivorship is, doctrinally, and the four common-law unities it traditionally requires.
- How joint tenancy is created in selected states — and why express survivorship language is required almost everywhere.
- What the joint tenancy does at death — and what the survivor receives mechanically and immediately.
- Six trade-offs of joint titling: will override, lifetime creditor exposure, partial basis-step-up loss, lost flexibility for blended-family planning, unilateral severance, and gift-tax / Medicaid look-back consequences.
- Tenancy by the entirety as the married-only variant, and community-property treatments in the nine community-property states.
- When joint tenancy is the right choice — and the five scenarios in which it is most often the wrong one.

Joint tenancy with right of survivorship is often described as simple and automatic.

In one sense, it is. When one joint tenant dies, the surviving joint tenant typically becomes the sole owner by operation of law — without court involvement, without probate, and without the will having any role in the transfer. The death certificate is recorded with the county recorder; an affidavit of survivorship may be filed; and the deed thereafter shows the survivor as the sole owner. The mechanic is administrative, not judicial.

But the simplicity comes with trade-offs. Joint tenancy:

- bypasses probate
- overrides the will
- collapses ownership into the survivor
- exposes the property to each co-tenant's creditors during life
- freezes the cost basis at the death of each successive owner only as to the deceased's share
- can be unilaterally severed during life by any joint tenant

Families often use joint tenancy without realizing that it eliminates flexibility, changes inheritance outcomes, and can unintentionally disinherit people the deceased meant to provide for. The transfer may be automatic, but the consequences are permanent.

What Joint Tenancy Is, Exactly

Joint tenancy is a form of co-ownership in which two or more persons hold a single, undivided interest in real property, with the distinctive feature that the death of one joint tenant causes the deceased's interest to vest immediately in the survivors. The doctrinal name for this is the right of survivorship — sometimes abbreviated JTWROS or simply WROS in deed practice.

Common-law tradition required four “unities” for a valid joint tenancy: unity of time (the interests must vest at the same moment), unity of title (they must come from the same instrument), unity of interest (they must be equal in size and duration), and unity of possession (each joint tenant must have an equal right to possess the whole). Modern statutes have relaxed some of these requirements in many states, but the basic principle survives: joint tenancy is a single, unified ownership held by multiple persons, and any of them can sever it during life by transferring their interest.

Table 3.1

State	Default presumption	Required language
California	Tenancy in common unless WROS expressly stated	"As joint tenants" or "with right of survivorship."
Florida	Tenancy in common unless WROS expressly stated	"As joint tenants with right of survivorship."
Texas	Tenancy in common; survivorship requires written agreement	Express survivorship agreement signed by both.
New York	Tenancy in common unless WROS expressly stated	"As joint tenants with right of survivorship."
Illinois	Tenancy in common unless WROS expressly stated	"As joint tenants with right of survivorship."
Pennsylvania	Tenancy in common unless WROS expressly stated	"As joint tenants with right of survivorship."
Nevada	Tenancy in common unless WROS expressly stated	"As joint tenants with right of survivorship."
Married couples in any state with TBE	Tenancy by the entirety presumed	Default if both grantees are spouses.

How joint tenancy is created in selected states (representative; consult current state law).

Two patterns in Table 3.1 are worth highlighting. First, in nearly every American jurisdiction the default presumption is against survivorship. A deed that simply names two grantees, without more, creates a tenancy in common — not a joint tenancy. To create a joint tenancy, the survivorship language must be expressly recited. Second, married couples in approximately half the states are presumed to take as tenants by the entirety — a married-only variant of joint tenancy with additional creditor protections during life. The presumption applies automatically unless the deed expressly directs otherwise.

What Joint Tenancy Does at Death

When a joint tenant dies, the deceased's interest does not pass through the estate. It does not appear in the inventory. The will does not address it. The probate court does not see it. Instead, the deceased's interest is extinguished, and the survivors' interests automatically expand to fill the space the deceased's interest had occupied.

Mechanically, this is implemented in the recording office by filing an affidavit of death of joint tenant (the title varies by state) together with a certified copy of the death certificate. The recorder updates the title chain to reflect the death; the surviving joint tenant or tenants are now the recorded owners. The entire process typically takes a few weeks and a recording fee of less than a hundred dollars.

There is no notice to creditors of the deceased. There is no creditor-claim window. There is no court approval. The property has moved from one set of hands to another by operation of law, and the law treats the transfer as complete the moment the death occurs.

The Trade-Offs

Six trade-offs of joint titling are worth understanding before any family chooses it as a planning device.

(1) The will is overridden. A joint-titled property is not controlled by the will, no matter what the will says. A parent who writes a will leaving the family home equally to three children, and who has joint-titled the home with one of the three, has — perhaps without intending it — disinherited the other two from any share of the house. We treat this in Chapter 9 in the context of family disputes.

(2) Lifetime exposure to co-tenant creditors. A joint tenancy interest is reachable by the personal creditors of any of the joint tenants. If a parent adds an adult child to the deed, and the child is later sued for negligence, divorces, or files bankruptcy, the child's interest in the parent's home becomes a target. This is the principal reason estate planners advise against putting an adult child on a deed as a joint tenant — even though it is one of the most common probate-avoidance shortcuts in folk practice.

(3) Loss of basis step-up on the surviving co-tenant's share. When any property owner dies, the federal income-tax basis of the deceased's interest is stepped up to the fair market value at the date of death. For property held jointly with a non-spouse, only the deceased's fractional share gets the step-up; the survivor's share retains its original basis. For property held in joint tenancy with a spouse in a non-community-property state, the same rule applies. For property held by spouses in a community-property state, both halves typically receive a full basis step-up — a significantly more favorable result. We treat

the basis question in Appendix M.

(4) Loss of flexibility for blended-family planning. Joint tenancy collapses the deceased's interest into the survivor's hands. The deceased cannot direct that, after the survivor's eventual death, the property pass to a particular person — a child from a prior marriage, a sibling, a charity. Once the joint tenancy operates, the survivor owns the entire property and can dispose of it however they choose, including by leaving it to a new spouse or to children the deceased did not know.

(5) Severance is unilateral. Any joint tenant can sever the joint tenancy during life by transferring their interest to themselves (usually as a tenant in common) or to a third party. The other joint tenants do not receive notice. The recorded severance is effective the moment it is recorded. Spouses contemplating divorce, co-investors in a souring partnership, and adult children frustrated by parental decisions all sometimes use this mechanism. It can be combative.

(6) Gift-tax and Medicaid-look-back consequences during life. Adding a non-spouse as a joint tenant on real property is treated, for federal gift-tax purposes, as a gift of half the property's value (or such other fractional interest as the parties intend). It triggers a gift-tax filing obligation if the value exceeds the annual exclusion. It also starts the Medicaid look-back clock — five years in most states — for any later application for long-term-care benefits. Families that add adult

children to deeds for probate-avoidance reasons sometimes discover, years later, that they have inadvertently disqualified themselves from Medicaid for five years.

> **KEY POINT**
>
> Joint tenancy with right of survivorship transfers property automatically at death, but the price of automation is the permanent loss of testamentary control. Once a property is held in joint tenancy, the will cannot direct its disposition; the survivor controls.

Tenancy by the Entirety: The Married-Only Variant

Approximately half the states recognize tenancy by the entirety, a form of joint tenancy available only to married couples. It functions much like joint tenancy with right of survivorship — the survivor takes automatically — but with two important additional features.

First, neither spouse can sever the tenancy unilaterally. Both must join in any conveyance, mortgage, or transfer. This protects each spouse from the other's unilateral action and from the other's creditors during life.

Second, the property is, in most TBE states, immune from the claims of creditors of one spouse only. A judgment creditor of the husband cannot attach the marital home held in tenancy by the entirety; the wife's interest is co-equal and cannot be impaired without her consent. This protection ends at the death of the first spouse — the survivor takes the entire property in their individual name and is then exposed to their own personal creditors — but during the life of both spouses it is meaningful.

Table 3.2

State	Recognized for real property	Notes
Florida	Yes	Strong creditor protection during marriage.
Pennsylvania	Yes	Recognized for real and personal property.
New York	Yes	Limited to real property.
Texas	No	Not recognized; community property regime.
California	No	Not recognized; community property regime.
Illinois	Limited	Limited to homestead property.
Nevada	No	Community property with right of survivorship available.
New Jersey	Yes	Recognized for real property.

Selected states recognizing tenancy by the entirety in real property (representative).

Community Property and Community Property With Right of Survivorship

Nine states are community-property states (Arizona, California, Idaho, Louisiana, Nevada, New Mexico, Texas, Washington, Wisconsin) and one (Alaska) permits opt-in community property by agreement. In these jurisdictions, property acquired by either spouse during marriage is presumptively community property, owned equally by both.

At the death of one spouse, community property is divided in half. The deceased spouse's half passes by will or by intestate succession; the surviving spouse retains the other half. The surviving spouse does not automatically take the deceased's half unless the will or community property with right of survivorship (CPWROS, an opt-in feature in some states) so directs.

The income-tax basis treatment of community property is particularly favorable. Both halves of community property — the deceased's and the survivor's — typically receive a full basis step-up at the death of the first spouse. This is the principal tax advantage of community-property titling and is one of the reasons spouses in community-property states should think carefully before retitling marital real estate as joint tenancy with right of survivorship — joint tenancy may produce only a half step-up where community property would have produced a full one.

Table 3.3

State	CPWROS available	Both halves stepped up at first death
Arizona	Yes (Ariz. Rev. Stat. §33-431)	Yes — IRC §1014(b)(6)
California	Yes (Cal. Civ. Code §682.1)	Yes — IRC §1014(b)(6)
Idaho	No statutory CPWROS	Yes — IRC §1014(b)(6)
Louisiana	No (civil-law forced heirship rules apply)	Yes — IRC §1014(b)(6)
Nevada	Yes (Nev. Rev. Stat. §111.064)	Yes — IRC §1014(b)(6)
New Mexico	Yes (NMSA §40-3-8)	Yes — IRC §1014(b)(6)
Texas	Yes (Texas Estates Code §112.001)	Yes — IRC §1014(b)(6)
Washington	Yes (RCW §64.28.040)	Yes — IRC §1014(b)(6)
Wisconsin	Yes (Wis. Stat. §766.60)	Yes — IRC §1014(b)(6)
Alaska (opt-in)	By community-property agreement	Yes — if validly elected

The nine community-property states (and Alaska's opt-in regime) — comparison of post-mortem treatment.

The double basis step-up under IRC §1014(b)(6) is the single most valuable tax feature available to spouses in these jurisdictions. It eliminates capital-gains exposure on the survivor's half as completely as on the deceased's half — a result that joint-tenancy titling cannot replicate in non-community-property states. Spouses in community-property states who later move to a non-community-property state can preserve the double-step-up treatment by taking title to subsequent property as community property in trust or by recording a community-property agreement before the move.

When Joint Tenancy Is the Right Choice

Despite the trade-offs, joint tenancy is often the right choice for married couples in their first marriage, with no children from prior relationships, who want the marital home to pass automatically to the survivor. The simplicity is real. The probate-avoidance is real. The override of the will is welcome rather than problematic, because the spouses' intent is identical: each wants the survivor to inherit. For this population, joint tenancy or tenancy by the entirety often is the correct titling.

The choice becomes more complicated in a few common scenarios:

- Blended families, where the spouses have children from prior marriages and want to ensure those children eventually inherit some share.
- Adult children added to a parent's deed as a probate-avoidance shortcut, where the planner usually loses more than they gain.
- Co-investors in a piece of real property, where the survivors-take-all rule conflicts with the parties' actual investment intent.
- Same-sex couples who married after long cohabitation and where the deed predates the marriage and may not have been

updated.

- Properties inherited by siblings or cousins as joint tenants from a common ancestor, who later disagree about disposition.

In each of these scenarios, the question is not whether joint tenancy is convenient — it always is, in the short term — but whether the loss of testamentary control and the exposure of the property to multiple sets of personal creditors are prices the parties actually understand and accept.

What This Looks Like in Practice

What This Looks Like in Practice

A father — call him Marcus — added his adult son, Jordan, to the deed of his free-and-clear $850,000 home in 2018, taking title as joint tenants with right of survivorship. The objective, as Marcus understood it, was probate avoidance. The mechanism was straightforward and inexpensive.

Three things happened over the next four years.

First, Jordan was sued for negligence in connection with his small landscaping business. The plaintiff obtained a judgment of $180,000. The judgment was recorded against Jordan's interest in his father's home — half of which Jordan now legally owned. The judgment lien clouded title and forced Marcus to choose between paying the judgment to clear the title or refinancing the property (which would now require Jordan's signature and a satisfaction of the lien).

Second, Jordan's marriage ended. The divorce court treated his interest in the father's home as a marital asset, requiring an offsetting payment to Jordan's ex-spouse to settle the property division. The settlement consumed Jordan's liquid savings and put additional pressure on his relationship with Marcus.

Third, when Marcus died in 2022, the home transferred automatically to Jordan as the surviving joint tenant. Marcus's will, which had attempted to leave the home equally to Jordan and his sister, had no effect — the joint tenancy overrode it. Marcus's daughter received no share of the home. The basis step-up at Marcus's death applied only to Marcus's half; Jordan retained the original carry-over basis on his half, producing significant capital-gains tax exposure when Jordan later needed to sell the property.

What had been intended as a simple probate-avoidance tool produced four problems: lifetime creditor exposure, exposure to a divorce property settlement, disinheritance of the daughter, and a partial basis step-up rather than a full one. Each was foreseeable. None had been foreseen.

The practical consequence of all of this is that families frequently arrive at the title company, after a death, to discover that the property they assumed would be theirs to direct has already moved — automatically, irrevocably, by operation of law — to a single survivor. The reverse also happens: families assume joint titling carried survivorship and discover, on review of the deed, that no survivorship language was ever included. In either case, the deed has spoken; the family is reading it for the first time.

Notes on Practice

The single most common practitioner observation about joint tenancy is that families consistently underestimate its permanence. The decision to add an adult child to a deed as a joint tenant — often presented as a casual probate-avoidance step — produces consequences that cannot be unwound without the child's cooperation. If the relationship later sours, if the child marries someone the parent dislikes, if the child predeceases the parent, the joint titling cannot be reversed unilaterally by the parent. For most adult-child planning, a transfer-on-death deed (where available) or trust ownership accomplishes the probate-avoidance goal without any of the lifetime entanglement.

A second observation: tenancy by the entirety, where available, is meaningfully better than ordinary joint tenancy for married couples. The additional creditor protection during life and the rule against unilateral severance both protect against scenarios that joint tenancy does not. In the states that recognize TBE, married couples should default to it for residential property.

Edge Case — The Predeceased Joint Tenant

A surprisingly common scenario in long-held joint tenancies: two co-owners take title in joint tenancy with right of survivorship in, say, 1985. One of them dies in 2003. The survivor never records an affidavit of death of joint tenant. The survivor lives in the property for another twenty years, treating it as theirs in every meaningful way — paying the taxes, maintaining the property, making improvements. On the survivor's death in 2026, the family discovers that title technically still names both the 1985 co-owners.

The cleanup is mechanical but irritating. The 2003 death must be documented to the recorder's office now — twenty-three years late — by filing the missing affidavit of death of joint tenant together with a certified death certificate. Once that filing is recorded, the chain shows the survivor as the sole owner from 2003 forward, and the 2026 estate can administer the property normally. The cost is small (a few hundred dollars in attorney fees plus recording fees), but the procedural delay can hold up an estate for several weeks.

The lesson: every death of a joint tenant produces an obligation to record an affidavit of death, even when the surviving co-owner has no immediate plans to sell. The cost is minimal; the simplification of any future transaction is substantial. Counsel handling estates should ask, as a standard intake question, whether any prior joint tenant died without the death being recorded against the property.

Edge Case — The Severance by Lender

A subtle and often overlooked source of joint-tenancy severance is the lender's customary deed-of-trust process. Most refinances, equity loans, and reverse-mortgage products require all owners to sign the security instrument. Some lender forms — particularly older ones — execute a transitional deed transferring title from the joint tenants to the trustee under the deed of trust. If the trustee's deed back to the original owners (recorded after the loan closes) does not expressly recite joint tenancy with right of survivorship, the original survivorship feature is destroyed and the parties become tenants in common.

This is rare in modern lender practice but appears often enough in older loan files that any refinance involving joint-tenant property should include explicit confirmation from the closing agent that the post-closing deed recreates the joint tenancy. Where the closing agent cannot confirm, a corrective deed restoring the joint tenancy should be recorded immediately. The fix is trivial. The discovery, post-mortem, that the family inadvertently lost survivorship during a routine refinance is not.

Common Questions, Briefly

Can a joint tenancy be created with the parties holding unequal shares?

Traditionally no. The four common-law unities of joint tenancy required equal interests as well as equal time, title, and possession. Modern statutes have relaxed this rule in some states (notably California and a handful of others), allowing joint tenancies with unequal shares expressly. In states that retain the common-law rule, a purported joint tenancy with unequal shares creates a tenancy in common in proportion to the recited shares, with the survivorship feature destroyed. The recording office accepts the deed either way; the legal effect depends on the state's version of the unity-of-interest rule.

What happens if all joint tenants die simultaneously?

Every state has a version of the Uniform Simultaneous Death Act addressing this scenario. Under the typical rule, where joint tenants die under circumstances making it impossible to determine the order of death, the property is administered as if each joint tenant survived the other for purposes of their respective shares — meaning the property is divided into proportional shares and each share passes through the respective decedent's estate. The joint-tenancy survivorship feature does not operate in simultaneous-death cases. This rule applies most often in automobile accidents, plane crashes, and other concurrent-death scenarios.

Practitioner Patterns — Joint Tenancy in Specific Settings

Three particular settings produce joint-tenancy patterns that deserve attention beyond the general framework. Each appears often enough in practice that families with the relevant facts should evaluate carefully whether joint titling is actually serving the goals they think it serves.

The first is the long-married couple in a non-community-property state. For these spouses, joint tenancy with right of survivorship (or tenancy by the entirety, where available) is usually the appropriate titling for the marital home. The survivorship feature ensures that the house passes immediately to the surviving spouse without probate; the simplicity is real and the trade-offs are minimal. The principal caveat is the basis-step-up treatment, which produces only a half step-up in non-community-property joint tenancy. For couples with significantly appreciated property — a long-held primary residence in an expensive metropolitan area — the lost step-up on the survivor's half can produce material capital-gains exposure when the survivor eventually sells. Where the appreciation is large, sophisticated planning may convert the ownership to a joint trust structure that produces full step-up while preserving the survivorship function.

The second is the elderly parent who adds an adult child as joint tenant for probate-avoidance reasons. This is the single most common joint-tenancy mistake in folk practice. The adult child's lifetime exposure (creditors, divorce, bankruptcy), the gift-tax filing obligation, the Medicaid look-back consequences, the partial basis-step-up, and the loss of testamentary control — all combine to make this structure substantially less attractive than the available alternatives. A transfer-on-death deed (where state law permits) accomplishes the probate-avoidance goal without any of the lifetime entanglement. A revocable living trust accomplishes the same goal with even more flexibility. Estate planners almost universally advise against parent-child joint titling for primary residences, and the reasoning has stood up across decades of subsequent litigation.

The third is the same-sex couple whose marriage was recognized later in life and whose home was titled before the marriage. For these couples, the deed often does not reflect either the modern marital relationship or the couple's actual intent about disposition at death. The cure is straightforward — a corrective deed during life that retitles the home in tenancy by the entirety (where available) or joint tenancy with right of survivorship — but the cure is rarely undertaken proactively. Counsel advising same-sex couples on estate planning should make the deed-review part of the standard intake; the correction is small, and the post-death consequences of leaving an outdated deed in place can be substantial.

Chapter 4 takes up the alternative: tenancy in common, the form of co-ownership that does not transfer automatically at death, and the form that produces most of the fractional-interest probate cases in American practice.

> **KEY POINT**
>
> Joint tenancy with right of survivorship transfers property automatically at death without probate, but the price of automation is the permanent loss of testamentary control. Once a property is held in joint tenancy, the will cannot direct its disposition; the survivor controls.

What This Chapter Has Said

Joint tenancy is a single, unified ownership held by multiple persons, with the distinctive feature that the death of one joint tenant causes the deceased's interest to vest immediately in the survivors. The mechanism is administrative, fast, and probate-free. The trade-offs — will override, lifetime creditor exposure, partial basis-step-up loss, lost blended-family flexibility, unilateral severance, and gift-tax / Medicaid look-back consequences — are real and permanent. Joint tenancy is often the right form for first marriages and frequently the wrong form for adult-child planning. Tenancy by the entirety adds creditor protection during life for married couples in the states that recognize it. Community property in the nine community-property states produces particularly favorable basis treatment but does not by itself produce automatic survivorship; CPWROS adds that feature where elected.

CHAPTER 4

Tenants in Common — When Ownership Splits Instead of Transfers

Chapter at a Glance

- What tenancy in common is, structurally — and why it is the default presumption in nearly every state.
- How tenancies in common arise: by inheritance, by co-investment, by default at conveyance, and by conversion from joint tenancy.
- Why the deceased's fractional share goes through the estate — and why this triggers probate the family did not anticipate.
- Three particularly common probate-triggering patterns: the intestate parent, the blended-family inheritance, and the investor co-tenancy.
- Partition as the absolute remedy of last resort — what it costs and what it forecloses.
- Where tenancy in common is the right structure, and how to retitle out of an unwanted one.

Tenancy in common ownership behaves very differently from joint tenancy.

When a tenant in common dies, the deceased's ownership interest does not transfer automatically. It becomes part of the estate. The interest passes by will, if a will exists, or by intestate succession if it does not. Probate may be required. Heirs may inherit fractional interests they did not anticipate. Disputes become more likely.

Many families discover tenants-in-common ownership only after the death, when multiple people suddenly own portions of the same property. The law treats this as normal. Families often do not.

What Tenancy in Common Is

Tenancy in common is the default form of co-ownership in nearly every American jurisdiction. When a deed conveys real property to two or more grantees without specifying the form of ownership, the default presumption — overcome only by express survivorship language — is that the grantees take as tenants in common. This is the rule that produces most of the surprise tenancy-in-common cases in American practice: the deed simply did not say otherwise.

Tenants in common share three principal features:

- Each co-owner holds a fractional, undivided interest in the entire property — a percentage that may be equal or unequal, fixed by the deed.

• Each co-owner has the right to possess and use the entire property, subject to the equal rights of the other co-owners.

• Each co-owner can transfer or encumber their fractional interest independently of the others, during life or at death.

There is no right of survivorship. The death of one tenant in common does not enlarge the interests of the others. The deceased's fractional share moves into the deceased's estate and is administered there.

How Tenancies in Common Arise

Most tenancies in common arise in one of four ways.

(1) Inheritance. The most common origin. When a property passes by will or by intestate succession to multiple heirs, those heirs take as tenants in common. A parent who dies intestate, leaving three adult children, produces three tenants in common, each holding a one-third interest in the parents' home. The parent did not choose this. The state's intestate-succession statute did.

(2) Co-investment. Friends, family members, or business associates who pool money to buy investment real estate frequently take title as tenants in common, sometimes with unequal interests reflecting their unequal contributions. Two cousins who buy a vacation property 60/40 are tenants in common in those proportions.

(3) Default at conveyance. As Chapter 3 noted, a deed that fails to specify joint tenancy creates a tenancy in common in nearly every state. Many older deeds — drafted before standard forms were computerized, or by parties who did not appreciate the distinction — created tenancies in common where joint tenancy was intended.

(4) Conversion from joint tenancy. As also noted, any joint tenant can unilaterally sever the joint tenancy during life by recording a deed transferring their interest to themselves as a tenant in common. This is sometimes done deliberately as a planning move and sometimes done inadvertently in the course of refinancing or transferring an interest to a trust.

Table 4.1

Feature	Joint tenancy (WROS)	Tenancy in common
Survivorship at death	Yes — automatic	No — share goes to estate
Probate required	No	Yes (for deceased's share)
Will controls deceased's share	No	Yes
Equal interests required	Traditionally yes	No — shares can be unequal
Each co-owner can transfer share	Yes (severs joint tenancy)	Yes (no severance issue)
Right to possess whole property	Yes	Yes (subject to others' equal rights)
Default presumption in most states	No (must be expressly stated)	Yes (default)
Federal estate-tax inclusion	Includes deceased's contribution share	Includes deceased's fractional interest
Basis step-up at death	Only on deceased's share (non-spouse) or per state	Only on deceased's fractional share

Joint tenancy versus tenancy in common — a side-by-side comparison.

What Happens at the Death of a Tenant in Common

When a tenant in common dies, the deceased's fractional interest becomes part of the estate. If the deceased had a will, the will directs disposition of the interest — to a spouse, a child, a trust, a charity, or any other beneficiary the will names. If the deceased had no will, the state's intestate-succession statute directs disposition.

In either case, the interest passes only after probate. The executor or administrator petitions the court, the court appoints, creditor claims are received, and — eventually — the court authorizes a deed transferring the deceased's fractional interest to the named beneficiary or beneficiaries. The recording office then shows the new co-owner alongside the surviving original co-owners.

If the will leaves the interest equally to three children, the result is that the three children become co-tenants with the original surviving co-tenants. The number of co-owners increases. Their fractional shares become smaller. Decision-making becomes more complicated. The phenomenon is well-known in property practice and is called heir-property fragmentation. We treat its consequences in Chapter 8.

The Three Common Probate-Triggering Patterns

Three particular patterns of tenancy-in-common ownership reliably produce probate proceedings that the family did not anticipate.

(1) The intestate parent. A parent dies without a will, owning the family home in their sole name. Under most state intestate-succession statutes, the home passes — depending on whether there is a surviving spouse and whether the children are also the spouse's children — to some combination of spouse and children. If the deceased was unmarried and survived by adult children, the home passes to the children equally as tenants in common. The children may or may not have known each other well. They are now co-owners of a single asset they cannot use without unanimity.

(2) The blended-family inheritance. A parent dies leaving the marital home to a surviving spouse for life, with the remainder to the children of the prior marriage. Or the will leaves the home outright to the surviving spouse, with a precatory wish that the spouse leave it to the deceased's children. Or the spouses held the home as tenants in common (rather than joint tenancy), and the deceased's share now passes by will to the deceased's children from the prior marriage — producing a tenancy in common between the surviving spouse (who occupies the home) and the deceased's stepchildren (who do not). These structures are flammable. We treat them in Chapter 9 and Chapter 12.

(3) The investor co-tenancy. Three friends pooled money to buy an investment property as tenants in common, equally. One dies. The deceased's one-third interest passes to the deceased's spouse (who has no interest in real estate investing) and the deceased's two children (one of whom does, one of whom does not). The surviving two original investors now find themselves in a co-tenancy with three new co-owners they did not select. Refinancing requires every co-owner's signature. Sale requires every co-owner's agreement. The investment that was once a three-way partnership is now a five-way negotiation.

Partition: The Last Resort

When co-tenants cannot agree on what to do with a jointly held property, every American jurisdiction provides a remedy of last resort: a partition action. Either physical division of the property (partition in kind) or a court-ordered sale with the proceeds divided according to the co-tenants' fractional interests (partition by sale).

Partition is an absolute right of any tenant in common. No other co-tenant can prevent it. The court will order partition even over the objection of co-tenants who wish to keep the property. The modern preference, in most jurisdictions, is for partition by sale, because most modern parcels — single-family homes, condominium units, commercial buildings — cannot be physically divided in any useful way.

Partition actions are slow, expensive, and emotionally costly. They typically take eighteen to thirty-six months. Attorneys' fees and costs are paid first from the sale proceeds, before any distribution to the co-tenants. The court appoints a referee or commissioner who supervises the sale, often by public auction, frequently producing a price below market. Family relationships rarely survive the proceeding.

Some states have enacted the Uniform Partition of Heirs Property Act (UPHPA), which provides additional protections for tenancy-in-common property that arose by inheritance — a right of first refusal for non-petitioning heirs, a court-ordered appraisal, a preference for open-market sale over forced auction. Approximately twenty-two states have adopted some version of the UPHPA as of writing. Even with the additional protections, partition remains the proceeding of last resort.

Table 4.2

State	UPHPA adopted	Default partition method
California	Yes (2022)	Sale preferred for residential; partition in kind for divisible parcels.
Texas	Yes (effective 2017)	Partition in kind preferred where feasible; sale otherwise.
New York	Yes (2019)	Sale typical for urban residential; partition in kind for rural land.
Florida	Yes (2020)	Sale by court-supervised auction; UPHPA right of first refusal applies.
Pennsylvania	Yes (2021)	Sale typical for residential; partition in kind for farmland.
Illinois	Yes (2019)	Sale preferred; partition in kind on showing of feasibility.
Nevada	Yes (2021)	Sale typical; UPHPA appraisal and right of first refusal apply.
Georgia	Yes (2012; pioneer state)	Sale preferred; UPHPA buy-out provision available.
South Carolina	Yes (2016)	Sale typical; UPHPA appraisal and buy-out heavily relied upon.
Ohio	No	Common-law partition; sale typical for residential.
Michigan	No	Common-law partition; sale typical for residential.
New Jersey	No	Common-law partition; sale typical for residential.

Selected states' partition statutes and UPHPA adoption status (representative).

The UPHPA changes the partition default in important ways. In a non-UPHPA state, a co-tenant who files for partition can force the property to public auction relatively quickly, frequently at a price meaningfully below open-market value. In a UPHPA state, the court must first obtain an appraisal, offer the non-petitioning co-tenants a right to buy out the petitioner's interest at the appraised value, and only then — if the buyout is declined — consider sale, with a statutory preference for open-market sale over forced auction. The result is meaningfully more co-tenant protection and meaningfully better proceeds. Inheriting families in heirs-property situations should always consult counsel familiar with the local UPHPA implementation, because the procedural advantages are real but waivable if not asserted in the early pleadings.

KEY POINT

Tenancy in common gives every co-owner an absolute right to force a sale through partition. There is no contractual way to permanently prevent partition; the right is statutory and cannot be waived. Co-tenants who plan to hold property together for the long term should use a different ownership structure — an LLC, a trust, or a partnership — that contains internal decision rules and exit mechanics.

How to Avoid the Surprise

The single best way to avoid the surprise tenancy-in-common is to review every recorded deed during life — for every property the family owns, in every state — and confirm that each one says what the family thinks it says. The review takes a few hours. The deeds are a phone call to the title company away. Counsel can review them in a single sitting.

Where the deed creates an unwanted tenancy in common, the cure is a re-titling deed: a new deed, signed by all current co-owners, expressly creating joint tenancy with right of survivorship, transferring the property to a trust, or assigning the property to an LLC. Each of these is a simple recorded conveyance, generally costing a few hundred dollars in legal fees and recording costs, and each of them produces a sharply different post-mortem outcome from the unrevised tenancy in common.

It is often the highest-value, lowest-cost piece of estate planning the family will ever do.

What Tenancy in Common Does Well

We have spent the chapter on the difficulties of tenancy in common because that is where the surprises live. It is worth ending on what tenancy in common does well.

Tenancy in common is the right structure when the co-owners explicitly want their interests to remain separate and inheritable. Investors who pool money to buy property and intend each share to pass to the investor's own heirs. Siblings who jointly inherited property and want to ensure each branch's share continues to descend within that branch. Business partners who do not want a death to convert the partnership into a different ownership. For all of these, tenancy in common is precisely the form that preserves what the parties intend.

It is also the right structure when the parties do not want the lifetime entanglement of joint tenancy — the gift-tax exposure of adding a non-spouse, the creditor-exposure of joint titling, the loss of unilateral control — but do want shared ownership. Tenancy in common gives each owner full lifetime control of their own share, including the right to transfer, encumber, or devise it without the others' consent.

What This Means Going Forward

What This Looks Like in Practice

Three siblings — call them Daniel, Elena, and Frank — inherit their parents' home as tenants in common, equally, when their mother's intestate estate is settled. The home is in a desirable suburb of Chicago and is worth approximately $480,000. There is no mortgage.

Daniel lives in the home and has lived there since graduate school; he had returned to help with his mother's last illness and had simply stayed. Elena lives an hour away and operates a successful small business; she would like the home sold so the proceeds can be invested. Frank lives in another state and is indifferent — he would prefer cash but does not want to force the issue.

Three years pass. Daniel continues to live in the home. He pays the property taxes ($7,200 annually), the homeowners' insurance ($1,800), and the utilities. He has performed approximately $14,000 of repairs over the three years. He has paid nothing to Elena or Frank for their interests.

Elena, frustrated, files for partition. The proceeding takes nineteen months. The court orders a sale at public auction. The house sells for $432,000, approximately ten percent below the open-market estimate at the time the petition was filed. Attorneys' fees consume $48,000. Daniel's contribution claim for taxes, insurance, and repairs is recognized at $39,000 (the court disallows $8,000 as cosmetic improvements). The net distributable amount is approximately $345,000, divided equally — $115,000 each, less Daniel's contribution credit, yielding $76,000 each to Elena and Frank and $193,000 to Daniel after the credit.

By the conclusion of the proceeding, Daniel had moved out (with two months' notice from the court-appointed referee), the house had been sold to a stranger at below-market value, and the three siblings were not speaking. Elena had received less than she would have received from a negotiated buyout in year one.

Frank had received less than he would have received from any settlement at any point. Daniel had received more than the others (because of the contribution credit) but had lost his home and his relationship with both siblings.

All of this was preventable with a written co-tenancy agreement entered into in the first month after the inheritance — an agreement that would have addressed Daniel's right to occupy, the rent (if any) he would pay, the schedule on which one or more siblings could buy out the others, and the formula for valuation. The agreement would have cost a few thousand dollars in legal fees. The partition cost the family forty-eight thousand and considerably more than that in lost relationships.

The remainder of the book will return to tenancy in common repeatedly. Chapter 6 will treat the three paths a house can travel after a death — and the tenancy-in-common path is one of them. Chapter 8 will treat the disputes that arise when fractional co-owners disagree. Chapter 9 will explore why those disputes are so often more painful than the underlying property is worth. Throughout, the structural fact will be the same: tenancy in common is the form that produces fractional ownership, and fractional ownership is the form that produces most of the post-mortem property litigation in this country.

Notes on Practice

The dominant practical observation in tenancy-in-common practice is that the families who get themselves into fractional-ownership trouble are usually the families who did not realize they had created a tenancy in common in the first place. The default rule — that any deed conveying property to two or more persons creates a tenancy in common unless joint tenancy is expressly stated — surprises clients almost daily. Where the client's intent was joint tenancy, the cure is a corrective deed adding the survivorship language. The opportunity to make the correction usually exists for years before anyone realizes a correction is needed; very few tenancies in common become problematic quickly.

A second observation: where multiple co-tenants intend to hold property together for the long term, no form of co-tenancy is the right answer. The right answer is an LLC, a trust, or a partnership — entities that contain internal decision rules and exit mechanics. Co-tenancy is for short-term holdings and for relationships in which each party fully accepts the right of any of them to petition for partition at any time.

The Heirs-Property Phenomenon

Heirs property — real estate held by tenants in common as the result of one or more prior intestate or partial estate administrations — is a category of unusual public-policy importance and unusual practitioner difficulty. It arises most often when a property has passed through multiple generations without formal estate administration: great-grandparents died intestate; their children inherited as tenants in common; some of the children also died intestate; their shares in turn passed to grandchildren as fractional interests; some of those grandchildren also died; and the result, by the third or fourth generation, is a property with dozens of fractional owners scattered across the country, many of whom have never met.

Heirs property is concentrated in particular communities — rural areas, agricultural regions, historically Black communities in the southern United States, indigenous communities in the southwestern United States — where informal succession patterns and lack of access to estate-planning counsel have produced multi-generational fractional ownership. The properties are particularly vulnerable to forced partition sales by speculators who purchase a single fractional interest and then file for partition, often acquiring the entire property at below-market auction prices.

The Uniform Partition of Heirs Property Act (UPHPA), promulgated in 2010 and now adopted in approximately twenty-two states, is a direct response to this pattern. Where applicable, the UPHPA requires the court to obtain an independent appraisal, offer the non-petitioning co-tenants a right to buy out the petitioner's interest at the appraised value, and — only if the buyout is declined — consider sale, with a strong statutory preference for open-market sale over forced auction. The cumulative effect is to give heirs-property families meaningful procedural protection while preserving the underlying right to partition.

Where multiple heirs-property generations have produced very small fractional interests, a related cure is a consolidation deed — a recorded instrument signed by all current fractional owners that consolidates ownership into a smaller number of larger shares (often into a single LLC owned by the family). The consolidation eliminates the fractional-ownership exposure to forced partition and provides a structured framework for future decision-making.

Common Questions, Briefly

If I want to sell my fractional interest, can I just transfer it to a buyer?

Yes. Each tenant in common has full lifetime control of their own fractional interest, including the right to sell it to a third party. The other co-tenants do not need to consent; they do not even need to be notified. The buyer takes the seller's exact fractional interest and steps into the seller's shoes as a co-tenant. Whether the price is fair is your business; the transaction itself is unrestricted.

Can co-tenants prevent a partition by contract?

Permanent waiver of the right to partition is generally unenforceable because the right is statutory and considered fundamental to co-ownership. Reasonable temporal restrictions — agreements not to partition for a defined period (commonly 5 to 10 years) — are usually enforceable. The cleanest way to achieve permanent partition protection is to convert the co-tenancy to an LLC or partnership ownership, where the entity (not the individuals) holds the real property and the individuals' interests in the entity are personal property governed by the entity's operating agreement.

Practitioner Patterns — TIC Beyond Inheritance

Tenancy in common arises in settings beyond the inheritance context that the chapter has emphasized. Three additional patterns deserve treatment because they account for a meaningful share of the difficult TIC matters in current practice.

The first is the unmarried-couple tenancy in common. Two people who buy a home together but who are not married — long-term cohabitants, business partners, friends pooling resources for a starter property — typically take title as tenants in common. The form serves the parties' intent well during life: each owns a defined fractional interest and can transfer or encumber it independently. But at death, the deceased's fractional share passes to the deceased's heirs (often family of origin), not to the surviving co-owner. Couples who intend the survivor to take should record a transfer-on-death deed (where available) or hold the property in a joint revocable trust whose terms direct the desired result. The deed alone, without supplement, produces an outcome the couple frequently did not intend.

The second is the family-business real-estate tenancy in common. A small business operates from real estate held by the founders as tenants in common. As the founders age and transition out, the property often becomes the most complicated piece of the succession plan. Each founder's fractional interest passes through their estate; the inheritors may have no business relationship with the operating business; the operating business may have a lease (or may not) with no clear renewal terms. Where the business and the real estate are linked, the cleanest long-term structure is to convert the real estate to LLC ownership and the business operating tenant to a long-term written lease — separating the real-estate succession from the business succession and giving each its own framework.

The third is the inherited-rental-property TIC. Multiple siblings inherit a property that was generating rental income for the deceased. The siblings now jointly own a small business — landlord obligations, tenant relationships, ongoing maintenance, tax filings — that none of them signed up to operate. Decisions about repair budgets, rent levels, tenant selection, and capital improvements must be made on the timeline of an active rental property, not on the timeline of leisurely sibling consensus. Conversion to LLC ownership with a clear management structure is usually the right move. Where conversion is not feasible, partition often becomes the eventual answer — typically within two to five years of the inheritance.

Part III takes up the third major ownership form — trust ownership — which produces a third and very different post-mortem path.

Figure 4.1

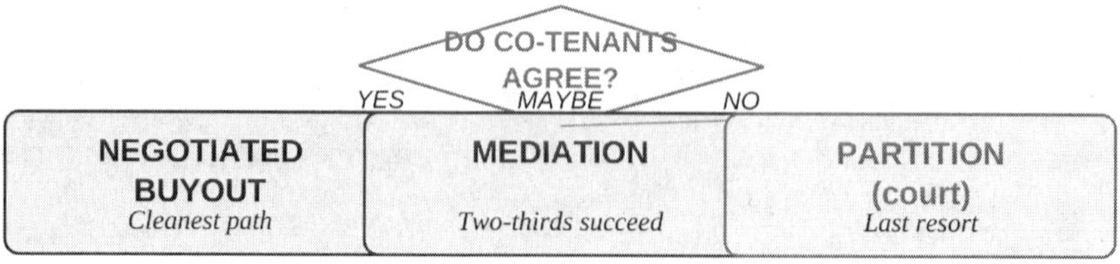

When co-tenants disagree — three paths forward, in order of cost and acrimony.

KEY POINT

Tenancy in common gives every co-owner an absolute right to force a sale through partition. There is no contractual way to permanently prevent partition; the right is statutory and cannot be waived. Co-tenants who plan to hold property together for the long term should use a different ownership structure — an LLC, a trust, or a partnership — that contains internal decision rules and exit mechanics.

What This Chapter Has Said

Tenancy in common is the default form of co-ownership in nearly every American jurisdiction. Co-owners hold fractional, undivided interests with no right of survivorship; the deceased's share passes through the estate. Most tenancies in common arise by inheritance, co-investment, default at conveyance, or conversion from joint tenancy. Each pattern produces probate of fractional interests and complicates subsequent decision-making. Partition is the absolute remedy of last resort and is always available to any co-tenant. Where co-owners want to hold property together for the long term, a more structured ownership form — an LLC, a trust, or a written co-tenancy agreement — is essential. Where the parties want their interests preserved as separate and inheritable, tenancy in common is precisely the form that produces that result.

PART III

TRUST-OWNED PROPERTY

What it really means for a trust to own a house — and how to tell whether yours actually does.

CHAPTER 5

Trust-Owned Property

Chapter at a Glance

- What a trust actually is, and what it means for a trust to own real property versus merely existing on paper.
- Why trust ownership avoids probate — because the deceased did not own the property; the trust did.
- The funding gap as the single most common failure in modern estate planning, and the six recurring patterns that produce it.
- How to verify, in five minutes, whether your trust actually owns your house.
- What the successor trustee does, in private, without court involvement.
- When a trust does not avoid probate — the unfunded asset, the pre-existing tenancy in common, and the surviving tort claim.
- What questions to ask your estate-planning attorney this week.

Property owned by a trust does not belong to the individual.

That sentence sounds simple. It is not. It is the foundation of modern estate planning, the source of most of its successes, and the source of nearly all of its quiet, unrecognized failures. Whether a particular property is or is not actually owned by a trust turns out to be one of the most consequential factual questions a family will ever investigate.

When property is properly titled in a trust:

- probate may be avoided
- ownership continuity is preserved across the death of the settlor
- transfer occurs under the trust's terms, not the will's
- creditor exposure may be reduced or restructured (depending on trust type)
- successor management is named in advance and steps in without court appointment
- privacy is preserved, because trust administration does not appear in any public docket

But the phrase "owned by a trust" matters. A trust that exists only on paper does nothing. A trust that actually holds title behaves very differently.

This distinction explains why some trust plans work and others collapse.

What a Trust Is, in Two Sentences

A trust is a legal arrangement in which one person (the trustee) holds title to property for the benefit of another person or persons (the beneficiaries), under terms set by a third person (the settlor or grantor) who created the trust. The trustee owns the property legally; the beneficiaries own it equitably; the settlor's instructions, written into the trust document, control how the trustee is to manage and eventually distribute it.

For most American families, the relevant trust is a revocable living trust — a trust the settlor can amend or revoke during life, in which the settlor typically serves as the initial trustee, and in which the settlor and the settlor's spouse (if any) are typically the initial beneficiaries. The trust becomes irrevocable at the settlor's death and a successor trustee, named in the document, steps in to administer the assets per the trust's terms.

When real property is owned by such a trust, the recorded deed names the trust (or, more precisely, the trustee in trust capacity) as the owner. A typical recital reads:

- "To Jane Doe, Trustee of the Jane Doe Revocable Living Trust dated January 1, 2020."

The legal owner is Jane Doe in her capacity as trustee. Jane Doe the individual does not own this property — Jane Doe the trustee does. When Jane dies, the named successor trustee — say, her daughter — steps into the trustee role and administers the property under the trust's terms. The deed does not need to be changed (the trust still owns the property) until the successor trustee eventually distributes the property to the trust's beneficiaries by recorded conveyance.

Why Trust Ownership Avoids Probate

Probate is the court-supervised process for administering an individual's estate after death. It applies to property the individual owned at death. Property owned by a trust is not owned by the individual — it is owned by the trustee in trust capacity, and the trustee did not die. The trust survives. Title does not need to be re-established because it never moved. The successor trustee simply continues administering the asset that the trust has owned all along.

This is why properly funded trust ownership avoids probate. The deceased did not own the property; the trust did. The probate court has no business with property the deceased did not own. The court is simply not involved.

KEY POINT

Probate is avoided not because the trust is special, but because the deceased did not own the property at the moment of death. Title was held by the trustee in trust capacity. The death of the settlor does not change the legal owner; it changes only who serves as trustee.

The Funding Gap — The Single Most Common Trust Failure

Here is where the system often breaks. The settlor signs the trust document — typically a forty-to-eighty-page instrument prepared by an estate-planning attorney — and the family assumes the work is done. The trust exists. The settlor's name is on the document. The successor trustees are named. The beneficiaries are listed. The tax provisions are sophisticated. The instrument is binding.

But the trust does not own anything until property is actually transferred into it. The signing of the trust document is a necessary first step. It is not a sufficient one. To make the trust own the family home, the settlor must also execute and record a deed transferring title from the settlor as an individual to the settlor as trustee. Without that recorded deed, the home remains in the settlor's individual name. The trust may be perfect on paper. The probate court, on the settlor's death, will still administer the home — because the home is still in the settlor's individual name on the recording page.

This is the funding gap. It is the single most common failure in modern estate planning. Surveys of practitioners consistently estimate that a substantial fraction — often cited at 30 to 50 percent — of revocable trusts have at least one major asset that the settlor never funded. The asset most commonly omitted is real property.

Table 5.1

Pattern	What happens	Why it happens
Trust signed; no funding deed prepared	Property remains in individual name; probate triggered at death.	Attorney drafted trust; no real-estate paralegal followed up.
Funding deed prepared; never recorded	Same outcome; the unrecorded deed has no effect against third parties.	Family forgot or lost the deed; the recording fee was never paid.
Property purchased after trust funding	New property in individual name; not in trust.	The settlor did not retitle at acquisition; broker did not raise it.
Refinance broke the funding	Lender required deed back into individual name; never re-funded post-closing.	Refinance is a common retitling-out moment that families forget to reverse.
Trust amended; deed not updated to reference new trust name	Trust may technically own property; recording chain shows old trust name.	Amendment changed trust formal name without recording a confirming deed.
Out-of-state property	Funded for in-state property only; out-of-state property left out.	Lawyer not licensed in second state; coordination never happened.

Why the funding gap happens — six common patterns.

How to Tell Whether Your Trust Is Actually Funded

Three documents, taken together, will answer the question of whether a particular trust actually owns a particular piece of real property:

1. **The trust document.** Confirms the existence of the trust, names the trustee and successor trustees, and identifies the trust by its full legal name and date. This is the source of authority but not the source of ownership.

2. **The deed.** Names the recorded legal owner of the property. If the deed shows the settlor in individual name, the trust does not own the property. If the deed shows the settlor (or any trustee) in trust capacity, with the trust's full legal name and date matching the trust document, the trust owns the property.

3. **A current title-company report or recent recording-office search.** Confirms that the deed shown is in fact the most recently recorded valid deed against the property. Older deeds that were prepared but not recorded, or that were superseded by later transactions, do not control.

All three should be examined together. Many families discover, on an annual review, that a trust they had assumed was complete is missing one or two assets — a vacation property, a piece of inherited farmland, the rental house bought after the trust was funded. The fix is the same as the original work: a deed from the individual to the trust, properly executed and recorded.

What the Successor Trustee Does

When the settlor of a revocable trust dies, the named successor trustee — typically the surviving spouse, an adult child, or a professional trustee — steps into the trustee role. The trust document itself is the source of the successor's authority; no court appointment is required.

The successor trustee's duties include:

- obtaining a tax-identification number for the (now irrevocable) trust,
- providing notice of the change of trustee to the beneficiaries,
- obtaining an appraisal or other valuation of trust assets as of the date of death,
- managing trust assets during the administration period,
- filing the trust's first annual income-tax return (Form 1041),
- paying the deceased settlor's debts as required by the trust agreement and applicable creditor-claim statutes,
- distributing trust assets to the beneficiaries per the trust's terms.

Notice that none of these steps requires court involvement. They are performed by the trustee, in private, under the trust agreement and applicable trust-administration statute. This is the principal practical difference between trust administration and probate administration: the same work happens, but in private, without a public docket, and on the trustee's calendar rather than the court's.

Distributing Real Property from a Trust

When the trust agreement directs that a particular property be distributed to a particular beneficiary, the successor trustee executes and records a trustee's deed transferring title from the trust to the beneficiary. The deed recites the trust as grantor and the beneficiary as grantee. It is a single recorded conveyance, generally completed in a few weeks at modest cost.

If the property is to be sold and the proceeds distributed, the successor trustee lists the property, executes the closing documents in trust capacity, and distributes the net proceeds per the trust's terms. The trust is the seller of record; the buyer takes from the trust; no probate court is involved at any step.

If the property is to remain in trust for the benefit of one or more beneficiaries — a common provision for spouses, minor beneficiaries, or beneficiaries with disabilities — the trustee simply continues to hold the property in trust capacity, administering it under the terms the settlor specified.

Trust Ownership and Federal Income-Tax Basis

Property held in a revocable trust receives the same basis step-up at the settlor's death as property held in the settlor's individual name. The trust is treated, for federal income-tax purposes during the settlor's life, as a grantor trust whose assets are deemed owned by the settlor. The settlor's death triggers the basis adjustment under Internal Revenue Code section 1014, and the property's basis is reset to its fair market value as of the date of death.

This is one reason to prefer revocable-trust ownership over, for example, gifting the property to children during life. A lifetime gift carries the donor's original basis (the carryover-basis rule of section 1015), often producing significant capital-gains tax exposure when the children later sell. A trust transfer at death produces a stepped-up basis, often eliminating decades of appreciation from the income-tax base. We treat the basis comparison in detail in Appendix M.

When a Trust Does Not Avoid Probate

Trusts do not always avoid probate. Three common situations trigger a probate proceeding even when a trust is in place.

(1) The unfunded asset. As discussed above. Any asset that the settlor failed to retitle into the trust during life is a probate asset. The pour-over will (a short companion will whose only function is to direct any unfunded asset into the trust at death) catches the asset, but the will must still be admitted to probate.

The pour-over saves the disposition. It does not avoid the proceeding.

(2) The pre-existing tenancy in common. If the settlor held a fractional interest in a property as a tenant in common, and transferred only that fractional interest into the trust, the settlor's death triggers no probate of the settlor's interest — the trust holds it. But if the property is later partitioned, the partition proceeding involves both trust and non-trust co-tenants. The proceeding itself is a court matter, even though the trust's share does not pass through probate.

(3) Tort claims and other survival actions. If the deceased settlor was the subject of a wrongful-death cause of action, an ongoing personal-injury claim, or any other claim that survives the settlor's death, that claim is administered by the deceased's estate — meaning a probate proceeding may be opened solely to prosecute or settle the claim, even if the trust holds all of the deceased's other assets.

REFLECTION

A trust does not eliminate the possibility of probate. It reduces the surface area where probate can attach, often to nearly zero. "Nearly" is not "none." The careful estate plan anticipates the small remainder and treats it as routine, not as failure.

What This Looks Like in Practice

Consider a settlor — call her Catherine — who set up a revocable living trust ten years before her death. The trust was drafted by a competent estate-planning attorney and named her two adult children as equal beneficiaries. Catherine signed everything. The attorney prepared a deed transferring the family home into the trust, and Catherine recorded it. The trust was funded as to the family home.

Five years later, Catherine inherited a vacation property from a sister. The estate-planning attorney was not involved in the estate of the sister; a different lawyer in a different state handled it. The deed transferring the vacation property to Catherine named her individually. Nobody told Catherine to retitle the vacation property into her trust. Nobody asked.

Three years after that, Catherine refinanced the family home. The lender insisted, as many lenders do, that title be transferred back into Catherine's individual name to clear the underwriting. Catherine signed the deed transferring the property out of the trust at closing. The trust attorney would have re-recorded a deed back into the trust after the refinance closed. But Catherine did not call the trust attorney. The deed back into the trust was never recorded.

Catherine died with two pieces of real property recorded in her individual name and a trust she believed owned everything. The successor trustee — her daughter — discovered the funding gap while reviewing the deeds in the first week. The result was a probate proceeding for both properties: the vacation property that had never been funded, and the family home that had been funded once but inadvertently un-funded at the refinance. The trust's careful tax provisions still controlled disposition; the pour-over will caught the residue. But the probate proceeding took fourteen months and cost the estate roughly nine thousand dollars in fees that a properly maintained funding plan would have eliminated entirely.

Catherine's case is unusually clean. Many funding gaps produce considerably more expense and considerably more delay. The lesson is the same: a trust funds itself only at the moment its assets are actually retitled. The plan is the easy part. The funding is the hard part.

What This Means for the Reader

If you have a trust, three questions are worth asking this week:

1. **Does the deed to my home, my vacation property, and any investment real estate I own actually name my trust as owner?** Pull the deeds from the recording office or call the title company. Confirm the recital matches the trust's exact legal name and date.
2. **Has any property changed hands in the past three to five years — a refinance, an inheritance, a new acquisition — without a follow-up retitling deed?** These

are the moments when funding gaps appear. They are the moments to address.

3. **Does my estate-planning attorney offer an annual review of trust funding?** Most do. Many do not perform it unless asked. Ask.

Forty-five minutes spent on these questions during life prevents weeks of probate work — and thousands of dollars in fees — after death. It is among the highest-leverage uses of an estate-planning attorney's time available to a family that has already completed the trust drafting.

Where We Go From Here

Notes on Practice

Two practitioner habits dramatically reduce trust-funding failures. The first is the annual review: every January, the settlor and counsel together review the deeds for every real property the settlor owns, against the trust's master schedule of assets, and confirm that each property is either in the trust or for an articulated reason out of it. The review takes less than an hour. It catches the great majority of unfunded assets within the year of acquisition rather than at death.

The second habit is the post-refinance follow-up. Whenever a settlor refinances a property held in trust, counsel automatically prepares a deed back into the trust to be recorded after the refinance closes. Treating this as a standard part of the refinance process — rather than a subsequent step the settlor must remember to request — eliminates one of the most common sources of inadvertent un-funding.

The Trust Funding Audit

A trust funding audit is a structured review, performed annually or whenever a major life event occurs (marriage, divorce, death of a settlor, large acquisition, refinance), that reconciles the trust's intended holdings against the actual recorded ownership. The audit produces a single page identifying each asset, its intended ownership, its actual ownership, and any corrective action required.

A complete trust funding audit covers at least six categories: real property (every parcel, by state and county), bank and brokerage accounts (every account, by institution), retirement accounts and life insurance (every beneficiary designation), business interests (every entity in which the settlor has an ownership stake), tangible personal property of significant value (art, jewelry, collectibles), and digital assets (cryptocurrency wallets, password vaults, intellectual property). For each, the audit asks two questions: is the current ownership what it should be? And if not, what instrument is required to correct it?

Estate-planning attorneys who offer this service routinely (often as part of an annual review fee) report that the audit catches a corrective need for one or two assets in the typical engagement — most commonly an after-acquired property, a missing beneficiary designation, or a deed that reverted to individual ownership at a refinance. Catching these errors during the settlor's lifetime, when they can be corrected by a simple recorded instrument, is the single highest-leverage estate-planning service available.

Edge Case — The Trust That Owns an LLC That Owns the Property

A common modern arrangement for investment real estate is for the property to be held in an LLC, with the LLC's membership interest held by a revocable trust. The structure provides liability protection (the LLC shields the trust from property-related liability), probate avoidance (the trust holds the LLC interest, so no probate of the underlying property), and ancillary-probate avoidance (the LLC interest is personal property governed by the law of the trust's situs, not the property's situs).

The structure works well when properly maintained, but requires three documents to be aligned: the deed (showing the LLC as record owner), the LLC operating agreement (showing the trust as the sole member), and the trust's schedule of assets (listing the LLC interest). When any of the three drifts out of alignment — typically because an amendment to one document was not reflected in the others — the structural integrity is compromised. Annual review of all three documents in tandem is essential.

Common Questions, Briefly

Does putting the house in the trust change my homestead exemption?

Generally no, in most states, provided the trust is a revocable living trust in which the settlor is also the beneficiary. The homestead exemption in most jurisdictions follows the property's use as the settlor's primary residence, not its formal title. Confirm with local counsel; a few states have technical requirements (specific trust language, recording of a homestead declaration naming the trust) to preserve the exemption. The verification takes minutes; the consequences of missing it (loss of property-tax savings, exposure to creditors) can be substantial.

If I die without ever amending my trust, does the trust still control?

Yes. The trust is a binding legal instrument from the moment it is signed and continues to control until amended or revoked. Most settlors review and amend their trusts every few years to reflect changes in family, finances, and law — but the absence of amendments does not impair the original trust's effect. The trust agreement that was in force at the moment of the settlor's death is the controlling document.

Practitioner Patterns — Trust Edge Cases

Beyond the funding-gap analysis that dominates this chapter, three trust-related patterns produce most of the complicated edge cases in current practice. Each is worth explicit attention because each is sufficiently common that any careful estate plan should anticipate it.

The first is the trust within a trust. Many modern revocable trusts include subtrusts that come into being at the settlor's death — credit-shelter trusts for tax planning, marital trusts for blended-family protection, special-needs trusts for beneficiaries on means-tested benefits, generation-skipping trusts for grandchildren. Each subtrust has its own administrative life: its own trustee, its own beneficiaries, its own tax filings, its own distribution rules. The successor trustee of the main revocable trust must understand not only how to administer the main trust but also how to fund the subtrusts and continue their separate administration. Where the original drafter is no longer available to explain the structure, the successor trustee should engage trust counsel for an early review of the entire trust architecture.

The second is the trust that has been amended multiple times. Trusts created decades before the settlor's death are often amended four, five, or more times to reflect changes in family circumstances, tax law, and the settlor's evolving intent. Each amendment is a separate instrument; the operative document at death is the trust agreement as last amended. Successor trustees inheriting a heavily amended trust should request and review the complete amendment history, because subtle inconsistencies between amendments can produce significant litigation. Where the amendments are voluminous, an amended-and-restated version (a single integrated document signed by the settlor that supersedes all prior amendments) dramatically reduces the administrative burden — and is an act of generosity toward future trustees.

The third is the irrevocable trust formed during the settlor's life. Some sophisticated estate plans use irrevocable trusts (irrevocable life-insurance trusts, qualified personal-residence trusts, dynasty trusts) to achieve specific tax or asset-protection goals. These trusts have their own administrative requirements during the settlor's life and continue after the settlor's death without the funding-gap risk that affects revocable trusts (the assets were transferred and cannot be withdrawn). The successor trustee's role is to continue administration per the trust's terms; the trust does not terminate at the settlor's death unless the document so directs. For families with substantial irrevocable trusts, the successor trustee's role is often a multi-decade fiduciary commitment that should be undertaken with full awareness of what it entails.

Part IV takes up what happens to a piece of real property at death — the three paths it can travel (Chapter 6) and the reasons it sometimes ends up in court despite the family's best planning

(Chapter 7). The path it travels depends entirely on the ownership structures we have now examined: individual ownership, joint tenancy, tenancy by the entirety, tenancy in common, and trust ownership. Each produces a different post-mortem story. Most families have a mix of all of them.

Figure 5.1

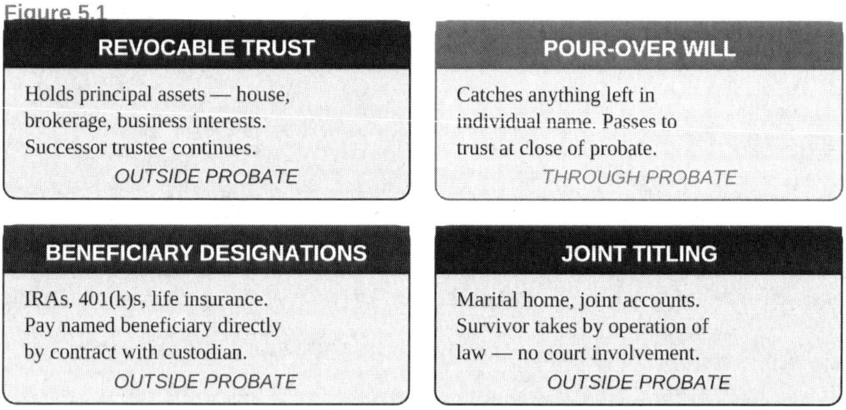

The trust ownership architecture — four parallel transfer mechanisms operating at death.

> **KEY POINT**
>
> A trust funds itself only at the moment its assets are actually retitled. The plan is the easy part. The funding is the hard part. Forty-five minutes of annual review prevents the great majority of trust-funding failures.

What This Chapter Has Said

Property owned by a trust does not belong to the individual; it belongs to the trustee in trust capacity. The settlor's death does not change the legal owner — it changes only who serves as trustee. This is why properly funded trust ownership avoids probate. The single most common failure in modern estate planning is the funding gap: the trust agreement is in place, but the deed still names the settlor individually. Six recurring patterns produce the gap; all of them are detectable in an annual review of the deeds. The successor trustee's authority comes from the trust agreement, not from a court order, and the proceeding is private. Trusts do not always avoid probate — unfunded assets, pre-existing tenancies in common, and surviving tort claims can each trigger court involvement — but a well-maintained trust eliminates probate for the great majority of property the settlor cared most about.

PART IV

◆

WHAT HAPPENS AT DEATH

The three paths a house can travel after a death — and the reasons it sometimes ends up in court.

CHAPTER 6

What Happens to the House at Death

Chapter at a Glance

- The three paths a piece of real property can travel after a death — automatic transfer, trust transfer, and probate transfer — and the deed-based criteria that determine which path applies.
- What automatic-transfer mechanisms are available in your state and what each one requires.
- The transfer-on-death deed phenomenon and the state-by-state landscape of recognition.
- Why probate is sometimes the right path, despite its time and cost — the creditor-claim cutoff and the judicial confirmation of title.
- Mixed cases — the property where some interests pass through trust transfer and others through probate.
- How to determine, in five minutes, which path your particular property will travel.

After a death, real property travels one of three paths. There is no fourth path. The three are:

1. **Automatic transfer.** By operation of law, the property passes outside probate to a named survivor, beneficiary, or co-owner. No court is involved.
2. **Trust transfer.** The property, owned by a trust, continues to be administered by the successor trustee per the trust's terms. No court is involved.
3. **Probate transfer.** The property, owned by the deceased individually or as a tenant in common, is administered by the executor or administrator under court supervision. The court is involved throughout.

Confusion arises when families assume one path applies and discover another does. The discovery usually happens at one of three particular moments: when the family tries to sell the house, when someone tries to refinance, or when a dispute arises. The law does not adjust to the family's expectations. It enforces the structure the deed already created.

Path One — Automatic Transfer

Several titling structures produce automatic transfer at death, without any court involvement. The deceased's interest moves directly to the named recipient by operation of the recording act, without a probate proceeding.

Table 6.1

Structure	What transfers	Mechanism
Joint tenancy with right of survivorship	Deceased's interest extinguished; survivor takes whole.	Affidavit of death of joint tenant; recording fee.
Tenancy by the entirety (married)	Survivor takes whole automatically.	Affidavit of death of joint tenant; recording fee.
Community property with right of survivorship (CPWROS)	Survivor takes whole; both halves get basis step-up.	Recording of CPWROS election plus death certificate.
Transfer-on-death deed (TOD deed)	Beneficiary named on TOD deed takes whole.	Beneficiary records death certificate and TOD-deed affidavit.
Lady-Bird deed (TX, FL, MI, VT, WV, NM)	Remainderman named in deed takes whole.	Recording of original Lady-Bird deed; recording of death certificate.
Life-estate deed	Remainderman takes; life estate ends at death.	Recording of original life-estate deed; recording of death certificate.

Titling structures that produce automatic transfer at death.

Each of these structures requires the right paper to have been recorded during life. The structure cannot be created post-mortem. A family that arrives at the recording office hoping to add a transfer-on-death designation after the owner has died discovers that the option no longer exists; the time for that decision passed when the owner did.

The Transfer-on-Death Deed Phenomenon

Approximately twenty-eight states recognize some form of transfer-on-death deed (or its functional equivalent — the Lady-Bird deed in five states, the "beneficiary deed" in others). These instruments allow the owner of real property to designate, on a recorded deed, who will take the property at the owner's death — without granting any present interest, without any creditor exposure, and without any need for probate. The owner retains complete control during life, including the right to revoke or amend the designation at will.

Where available, the transfer-on-death deed is one of the most useful probate-avoidance tools in the field. It is inexpensive (typically a few hundred dollars in legal fees plus a recording fee), revocable at any time, and produces an automatic transfer outside probate that a family-acquaintance witness need not even notarize. The principal limitations are jurisdictional: the deed must be recognized in the state where the property is located, and the deed must be executed and recorded with the formalities the state requires.

Table 6.2

State	Statutory authority	Notable features
California	Cal. Prob. Code §5600 et seq.	Beneficiary takes subject to debts; statutory form.
Nevada	Nev. Rev. Stat. Ch. 111	Statutory form; beneficiary deed.
Illinois	765 ILCS 27/	Comprehensive transfer-on-death instrument act.
Texas	Texas Estates Code §114	Texas Real Property Transfer on Death Act; statutory form.
Florida (Lady-Bird only)	Common-law enhanced life estate	Reserved life estate plus power to convey.
New York	Not recognized	Use trust ownership instead.
Pennsylvania	Not recognized	Use trust ownership instead.
Ohio	ORC §5302.22	Transfer-on-death designation affidavit.

Selected states recognizing transfer-on-death deeds (representative; consult current state law).

Where transfer-on-death deeds are not available, the functional equivalent is trust ownership — placing the property in a revocable trust during life and naming the eventual beneficiary in the trust agreement.

Path Two — Trust Transfer

Property owned by a trust at death continues to be owned by the trust after death. The death of the settlor does not transfer title; it transfers trustee authority. The successor trustee, named in the trust agreement, steps into the trustee role and administers the property under the trust's terms. There is no court involvement; the trust agreement is the source of authority.

Chapter 5 treats trust ownership in detail. The principal points for purposes of Path Two are:

- The deed must show the trust as the recorded owner. If it does not, the property is on Path Three (probate), regardless of what the trust agreement says.
- The successor trustee's authority comes from the trust agreement, not from a court order. No Letters Testamentary are required.
- Distribution to the trust's beneficiaries is by trustee's deed — a single recorded conveyance, executed by the successor trustee in trust capacity.
- The proceeding is private. Nothing about the trust administration appears in any public docket.

Trust transfer is the cleanest of the three paths when it is available. The principal failure mode is the funding gap — the asset that should have been on Path Two but was never retitled into the trust, and is therefore on Path Three instead.

Path Three — Probate Transfer

Property owned by the deceased individually, or held as a tenant in common with no survivorship feature, falls onto the probate path at death. The court appoints an executor or administrator, issues Letters Testamentary or Letters of Administration, and supervises the orderly transfer of title.

The probate path's mechanics for real property are largely the same as for any other probate asset, but with a few real-property-specific features:

1. **Inventory and appraisal.** Real property must be appraised as of the date of death. The appraisal becomes the property's tax basis going forward and is filed with the court.
2. **Notice and creditor-claim period.** The same creditor-claim window that applies to other estate assets applies to real property. Property cannot be sold or distributed before the period closes (or, in some states, before specific court authorization).
3. **Sale or distribution.** If the property is to be sold, the executor lists it (often with court approval) and conducts the sale under any applicable court-supervision rules. If the property is to be distributed in kind to one or more beneficiaries, the court issues an order confirming the transfer, and an executor's deed is recorded.

4. **Closing of the estate.** After distribution and accounting, the court approves the final accounting and discharges the executor. Title to the real property is now firmly in the beneficiaries' hands.

The probate path takes the longest. In an uncontested case of ordinary complexity, eight to twelve months from death to distribution. In a contested case, two to four years. Companion volume Probate Explained (AVOY, 2026) treats the probate calendar in detail.

Why Probate Is Sometimes the Right Path

Probate is often described as something to be avoided. For real property, it sometimes is. But not always. Probate offers two structural features that the alternative paths do not:

First, the creditor-claim cutoff. Probate establishes a publicly noticed window during which any creditor of the deceased must present claims against the estate; claims not presented in the window are time-barred. Trust administration does not always produce the same finality. Where a deceased owner had significant creditor exposure, probate's claim-cutoff can be a feature, not a bug.

Second, judicial confirmation of title. The probate court's order distributing real property to a beneficiary is, in most states, conclusive on the question of title. The beneficiary takes a court-confirmed title. A trust's deed, while perfectly valid, sometimes raises title-insurance underwriting questions (particularly where the trust was amended multiple times during the settlor's life and the recorded chain does not perfectly track the amendments). The probate path produces a slightly cleaner subsequent title chain in some cases.

Most families do not need either of these features and would rather avoid the probate proceeding's time and cost. But the categorical claim that probate is always to be avoided is incomplete. The right path depends on the family's circumstances.

Mixed Cases — When a Property Travels Two Paths

Some properties travel two paths simultaneously. The classic example is the property held as tenants in common where some interests are in trust and others are not. When the trust holder dies, that interest passes by trust transfer (Path Two). When a non-trust co-tenant later dies, that interest passes by probate transfer (Path Three). The property is now co-owned by the trust (through its successor trustee) and by the deceased non-trust co-tenant's heirs (through probate).

Mixed-path properties are the most common source of post-mortem real-property litigation. The interests are real, the recorded title is fragmented, and the procedural paths through which the fragments arrived are different. We treat the conflicts that follow in Chapter 8.

KEY POINT

Every parcel of real property at death travels one of three paths: automatic transfer, trust transfer, or probate transfer. Which path applies depends entirely on the deed's form of ownership at the moment of death. The path cannot be changed retroactively.

How to Predict Which Path Applies

For any particular property, the path is determinable in five minutes:

1. **Pull the most recently recorded deed against the property.** Any title company or county recorder's office can produce it.
2. **Read the form-of-ownership recital.** Sole ownership; joint tenancy; tenancy in common; tenancy by the entirety; trust ownership; or some combination.
3. **Identify any transfer-on-death overlay.** A recorded TOD deed, beneficiary deed, or Lady-Bird deed naming a remainderman.
4. **Determine the deceased's role at the time of death.** Sole owner; surviving joint tenant; surviving tenant by the entirety; or trustee of a trust holding title.
5. **Apply the path rules.** Automatic transfer (Path One) if joint tenancy, tenancy by the entirety, CPWROS, TOD, Lady-Bird, or life estate; trust transfer (Path Two) if trust ownership; probate transfer (Path Three) if sole ownership

or tenancy in common.

Five minutes of deed review answers the question for most properties most of the time. The complication arises only when the deeds are missing, the recording chain is broken, or the property is in a state with unusual rules (community-property states, states recognizing tenancy by the entirety in unusual ways). For these, professional title work is needed. The cost is small; the certainty is large.

What This Looks Like in Practice

Consider a single estate — that of Mrs. Whitman, an eighty-six-year-old widow who died with three pieces of real property: her primary residence in Phoenix, a vacation cabin in Flagstaff, and a one-quarter interest in her late husband's family farm in Iowa. Each property travels a different path.

The Phoenix home was titled in Mrs. Whitman's revocable trust. The trust was funded properly when it was created in 2014. The successor trustee — Mrs. Whitman's daughter — accepts the trustee role within two weeks of death. The trustee continues to administer the property. Within four months, the property is distributed to the daughter by trustee's deed, recorded in the Maricopa County recorder's office. Path Two — trust transfer.

The Flagstaff cabin was held in joint tenancy with right of survivorship between Mrs. Whitman and her son. On Mrs.

Whitman's death, the cabin transfers automatically to the son. He records an affidavit of death of joint tenant together with a certified death certificate at the Coconino County recorder's office. The transfer is complete within three weeks of death. Path One — automatic transfer.

The Iowa farm interest was titled in Mrs. Whitman's individual name (a tenancy-in-common interest she had inherited from her husband twenty years before and had never put into the trust). The interest is a probate asset, in Iowa, in a state where Mrs. Whitman did not reside. An ancillary probate proceeding is opened in Iowa. The proceeding takes nine months and costs the estate approximately $7,500 in legal and court fees. Path Three — probate transfer (in this case, ancillary).

Same estate. Three properties. Three paths. The choice of path was made decades before death, by the form of ownership chosen at each property's acquisition or last retitling. The Phoenix path was the cleanest — six weeks. The Flagstaff path was the fastest — three weeks. The Iowa path was the most expensive and the slowest — nine months and several thousand dollars. None of these outcomes was unusual; all of them were predictable from reading the deeds.

Where We Go From Here

Notes on Practice

Three practical observations are worth recording about the three-paths framework. First, mixed-path estates are far more common than single-path estates. Most deceased Americans leave behind some property on Path One (a joint marital home), some on Path Two (a trust-funded investment account), and some on Path Three (the unfunded asset, the inherited interest, the recently acquired vacation property). The administration of a typical estate involves all three paths simultaneously.

Second, the path that takes the longest is usually the path no one expected. Families plan around the trust, anticipate the joint tenancy, and are then surprised by the small probate proceeding for the asset nobody remembered. Annual review of the deeds — for every parcel, in every state — is the single most effective intervention against this pattern.

The Hidden Path-Three Asset

A particular sub-pattern deserves explicit attention. Families often discover, weeks or months into an estate administration, an unexpected real-property interest that must be administered through probate even though everything else is on Paths One or Two. The most common categories:

- A mineral interest, oil-and-gas royalty interest, or timber-rights interest the deceased inherited from a parent or grandparent and never integrated into their estate plan. These interests are real property, are typically held individually, and require formal probate to transfer.

- A fractional interest in a vacation home held with siblings or cousins. The deceased's fractional share is a probate asset even when the property's overall ownership is among trust-holding co-tenants.
- A long-forgotten interest in a family farm or rural land, often acquired by intestate succession decades earlier, never developed and never sold.
- A burial plot or cemetery interest. Yes, these are real property. They typically require probate to transfer, even though the financial value is modest.
- A property received as security for an old loan that the borrower never repaid. The security has technically vested but was never affirmatively conveyed.
- A leasehold interest of unusual length (a 99-year ground lease, a long-term commercial lease) — these are real-property interests in many jurisdictions and require probate-style transfer at the leaseholder's death.

The practical recommendation: every executor or successor trustee, in the first thirty days, should request a comprehensive title search not only on the deceased's primary residence but also on every property the deceased ever owned an interest in — including any properties inherited, gifted, or otherwise acquired and possibly forgotten. The cost is modest (a few hundred dollars per county). The discoveries can be material.

Edge Case — The Property Held in Multiple Capacities

Some properties are held in more than one capacity at once — a frequent source of confusion at death. Examples:

- Property held by the deceased as trustee for someone else's trust. The deceased held legal title; the beneficial interest belongs to the other trust's beneficiaries. The property does not belong to the deceased's estate; it remains with the successor trustee of the other trust.
- Property held by the deceased as custodian under UTMA for a minor. Same analysis: the property belongs to the minor; the deceased was merely the custodian. The successor custodian named in the original UTMA designation steps in.
- Property held by the deceased as guardian of a ward's estate. The property belongs to the ward; the deceased was the court-appointed guardian. The probate court must appoint a successor guardian.
- Property held by the deceased as agent under a power of attorney. The property belongs to the principal; the deceased's authority ended at the deceased's death. The principal (if still alive) regains direct control.

In each case, the property is recorded under the deceased's name but does not belong to the deceased's estate. The successor in the relevant fiduciary capacity takes over administration; the deceased's executor has no role. Recognizing these patterns early prevents months of wrong-tracked administration and the embarrassment of discovering that the deceased's estate has no claim to property the family had assumed was the deceased's.

Common Questions, Briefly

If I record a transfer-on-death deed and then later sell the property, what happens to the TOD designation?

The sale supersedes the TOD designation. A TOD deed operates only on whatever interest the grantor still owns at death. If the property has been sold during the grantor's life, the TOD designation has no operative effect because the grantor no longer owns the property to transfer. The TOD beneficiary takes nothing. The recorded TOD deed becomes a historical artifact in the title chain but does not impair the buyer's title.

Can I name multiple beneficiaries on a TOD deed?

Yes, in every state that recognizes TOD deeds. The beneficiaries take as tenants in common in proportions specified in the deed (or equally if no proportions are stated). Most TOD-deed statutes also allow successive beneficiaries — alternates who take if the primary beneficiary predeceases the grantor.

Practitioner Patterns — Path Selection in Real Time

The three-paths framework presented in this chapter is descriptive — it tells you what path applies to a particular property after the death has occurred. The more interesting question, and the one that makes estate planning worthwhile, is the prescriptive one: which path should a particular property be on, given the owner's actual circumstances and goals? Three considerations dominate the decision.

The first consideration is privacy. Path Three (probate) produces a public proceeding in which the will, the inventory, and the accounting all become matters of public record. For most families, this is acceptable; the public proceedings are rarely scrutinized by anyone outside the family. For families with privacy-sensitive considerations — public profiles, complex business holdings, family disputes that would be embarrassing if litigated publicly — Paths One and Two are sharply preferable. Trust ownership in particular produces complete privacy: nothing about the trust's administration appears in any public docket.

The second consideration is finality of creditor exposure. Path Three produces a publicly noticed creditor-claim window; claims not presented in the window are time-barred. This finality is genuinely valuable for estates with significant or uncertain creditor exposure — business owners who may face post-death claims, professionals who may face malpractice claims, families with disputed debts. Trust administration does not always produce the same finality, and depending on the state, creditors may have years to assert claims against trust assets. For estates where creditor finality matters, the small probate proceeding triggered by a pour-over will may actually be a feature rather than a defect.

The third consideration is family complexity. Simple families — long married, children all from the current marriage, no prior estranged relationships — can use any of the three paths comfortably. Complex families — second marriages with children from prior relationships, estranged children, beneficiaries with disabilities, non-marital partners — typically benefit from the drafting flexibility of Path Two (trust). The trust agreement can address contingencies and conditional distributions in ways that the deed (Path One) and the will (Path Three) cannot match. For these families, trust ownership of the principal real-property assets is usually the right structural choice.

Chapter 7 takes up the question of why properties get pulled into court even when the family expected they would not — the specific structural failures that account for most surprise probate proceedings involving real property.

Figure 6.1

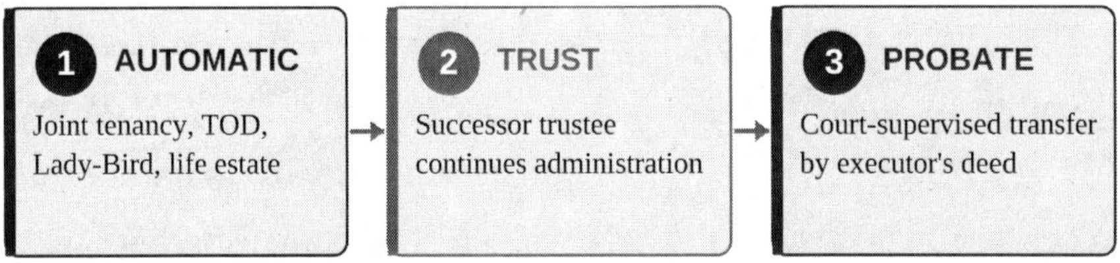

The three paths a piece of real property can travel after a death — automatic, trust, or probate.

KEY POINT

Every parcel of real property at death travels one of three paths: automatic transfer, trust transfer, or probate transfer. Which path applies depends entirely on the deed's form of ownership at the moment of death. The path cannot be changed retroactively.

What This Chapter Has Said

Real property after death travels one of three knowable paths. Automatic transfer (joint tenancy, TBE, CPWROS, TOD deed, Lady-Bird deed, life estate) requires no court involvement and resolves in a few weeks. Trust transfer (property owned by a properly funded trust) is private and resolves in three to twelve months. Probate transfer (sole ownership or tenancy in common) requires court supervision and resolves in eight to twelve months for uncontested cases. Probate is sometimes the right path despite its time and cost, because of the creditor-claim cutoff and the judicial confirmation of title. Mixed cases — where different interests in the same property travel different paths — produce most of the post-mortem real-property litigation. The path is always determinable in five minutes from the deed itself.

CHAPTER 7

Why Some Houses Get Pulled Into Court

Chapter at a Glance

- The six recurring patterns that pull houses into court: improper titling, outdated deeds, incomplete trust funding, conflicting ownership claims, multi-state property, and tort or specific-performance claims.
- Why improper titling — the deed that does not say what the family thought it said — is the single most common pattern.
- Three classic outdated-deed scenarios: the predeceased joint tenant, the dissolved marriage, and the amended-trust mismatch.
- Three sub-patterns of incomplete trust funding that are routinely overlooked.
- Why ancillary probate is the principal cost driver of multi-state property — and three approaches that reduce or eliminate it.
- How tort and specific-performance claims pull property into court even when the property's titling would otherwise

have avoided probate.

Even when families expect to avoid probate, houses can be pulled into court. The specific reasons are knowable. The recurring patterns are few in number.

Six recurring patterns account for the great majority of post-mortem real-property court proceedings:

1. **Improper titling.** The deed prescribes a form of ownership the family did not intend or did not understand.
2. **Outdated deeds.** Title still names a former joint tenant who predeceased the current decedent, or names a trust that has since been amended.
3. **Incomplete trust funding.** The trust agreement is in place; the deed still names the settlor individually.
4. **Conflicting ownership claims.** Two or more parties believe they hold the same interest; the recording chain does not unambiguously resolve the question.
5. **Multi-state property.** Property recorded in a state other than the state of the deceased's domicile triggers ancillary probate.
6. **Tort or specific-performance claims.** Claims that survive the death of the property owner — wrongful-death, contract, partition — must be administered in court even when the property itself transferred outside of probate.

This feels like a failure when it happens. Often it is simply exposure of an issue that existed for years.

Pattern One — Improper Titling

The single most common pattern is also the simplest. The deed did not say what the family thought it said.

A surviving spouse arrives at the title company believing the marital home was held in joint tenancy with right of survivorship. The deed shows tenancy in common. The deceased's half is now an estate asset. Probate is required to clear title.

An adult child believes they were added to the parents' deed as a joint tenant for probate-avoidance purposes. The deed shows the parents conveyed only a fractional interest, as tenants in common, with no survivorship language. Half the house is the child's; the parents' half passes through their estate.

A blended-family second-marriage couple believes they own the marital home as tenants by the entirety. The deed predates the marriage and was never updated. The recorded ownership reflects a tenancy in common created at the original purchase. The second-spouse co-tenant's share now passes by will or intestacy to the second spouse's children, not to the surviving spouse.

Each of these scenarios produces a probate proceeding that would have been avoided by a single corrective deed during life.

The cure is small. The discovery is uncomfortable.

Pattern Two — Outdated Deeds

Title chains accumulate. A deed recorded in 1972 between two joint tenants is still the operative ownership document if no subsequent deed superseded it. Most titles are layered — the current state of ownership is the cumulative result of every recorded conveyance in the chain. When one of those conveyances predates a death, a marriage, a divorce, or a trust amendment that nobody followed up on, the recorded ownership is what the deed says, not what the family assumes.

Three particularly common outdated-deed patterns:

1. **The predeceased joint tenant.** Two siblings took title in 1990 as joint tenants. One died in 2004; nobody recorded the death. The surviving sibling lived in the house, paid the taxes, treated it as theirs. On the survivor's death in 2026, title is technically in both names — the dead sibling's interest must be cleared first by a 2004 affidavit-of-death-of-joint-tenant filing, then the surviving sibling's interest must be administered through 2026 probate. Two sets of paperwork; the first one is twenty-two years late.

2. **The dissolved marriage.** Two spouses took title in 1985 as tenants by the entirety. They divorced in 2002 and recorded a divorce decree but no subsequent deed. Under

most state TBE statutes, divorce automatically converts a tenancy by the entirety into a tenancy in common. Title is now held by the ex-spouses as tenants in common. On the death of one in 2026, the deceased's half passes through the deceased's estate — to people the surviving ex-spouse may have had no relationship with for two decades.

3. **The amended-trust mismatch.** A settlor signed a trust in 2010 and recorded a deed transferring property to “the John Smith Revocable Living Trust dated January 1, 2010.” In 2018, the settlor amended and restated the trust, producing “the John Smith Revocable Living Trust dated January 1, 2010, as Amended and Restated October 5, 2018.” The deed was not updated. The recorded title still names the original trust. The successor trustee must now resolve, in some states by court petition, whether the original trust or the amended trust controls — typically with a relatively simple court order, but a court order nonetheless.

Pattern Three — Incomplete Trust Funding

Treated at length in Chapter 5. The settlor signed a trust. The trust was funded as to some assets and not others. The unfunded asset — typically real property — falls into probate at death. The pour-over will catches the disposition (sending the asset back to the trust at the close of probate), but the probate proceeding still happens.

Three particular sub-patterns are worth flagging because they are so frequently overlooked:

- Property acquired after the trust was funded. The settlor inherited or purchased the property after the original funding wave; nobody retitled it.
- Property re-titled out of the trust during a refinance. The lender required individual ownership; the trust attorney was not consulted; the deed back into the trust was never recorded.
- Out-of-state property. The trust attorney was licensed in only one state; the out-of-state property required local counsel; nobody coordinated.

Pattern Four — Conflicting Ownership Claims

Sometimes the recording chain itself is ambiguous. Multiple parties produce documents purporting to show ownership of the same interest in the same property. The court is the only forum that can resolve the conflict.

Common scenarios include:

- Two competing wills, each devising the same property to a different beneficiary, both purporting to be the deceased's last will.
- A recorded deed and an unrecorded deed, both purporting to convey the same interest, executed at different times by the same grantor.
- A deed signed under suspected undue influence, where the family of the original grantor disputes the validity of the conveyance.
- An adverse-possession claim, in which a long-term occupant asserts that years of open and hostile use have ripened into title.
- A boundary dispute, where the recorded legal description does not match the historical use of the land.

Each of these is a quiet-title or partition action waiting to be filed. None of them can be resolved by negotiation alone if the parties refuse to agree; the court is the institution of last resort. Where the dispute is real, the court is the right forum. Where the dispute is more about emotion than title, the court is unfortunately also the only forum, and it is an expensive one.

Pattern Five — Multi-State Property

When the deceased owned real property in a state other than the state of the deceased's domicile, the foreign-state property typically requires its own probate proceeding — known as ancillary probate — in addition to the principal probate proceeding in the state of domicile.

Ancillary probate is not optional. Real property is governed by the law of the situs (the location of the property), and only the courts of the situs state have jurisdiction to direct a transfer of recorded title. The domiciliary state's probate court can direct the executor to take steps to transfer the out-of-state property, but the ultimate recording of the deed must occur in the situs state, typically pursuant to an ancillary proceeding.

Three approaches reduce or eliminate ancillary probate:

1. **Transfer the out-of-state property into a revocable trust during life.** The trust holds the property; the death of the settlor does not change the legal owner; no probate (ancillary or otherwise) is required. This is the most reliable approach.

2. **Record a transfer-on-death deed in the situs state.** Where the situs state recognizes TOD deeds, this avoids ancillary probate by routing the property through automatic transfer at death.

3. **Hold the out-of-state property through an LLC owned by the trust or by the family.** The LLC holds the

real property; the family member's interest is in the LLC (a personal-property interest), not in the real property itself. The interest passes by the domiciliary state's probate proceeding (or by the trust agreement, if the LLC interest is held in trust). No ancillary probate is required.

Each of these approaches takes a few hours of attorney time and a recording fee. Each saves tens of thousands of dollars of ancillary probate cost over the long term. The economics are lopsided in favor of pre-death planning.

Pattern Six — Tort and Specific-Performance Claims

Some claims survive the death of the property owner and require court administration regardless of the property's titling. The principal categories are:

- Wrongful-death and survival actions — claims that arise from the deceased's injury or death.
- Specific-performance claims on real-property contracts the deceased had entered into but not closed (a sale contract, a lease option, a right-of-first-refusal exercise).
- Partition actions filed by co-tenants, which require court supervision regardless of how each co-tenant's interest was originally titled.
- Quiet-title actions to resolve clouds on title that the deceased had not addressed during life.

- Adverse-possession claims by long-term occupants, which (where successful) re-title property by judicial decree.

These court proceedings are not technically probate, but they function as probate in their effect on the deceased's real property: the property cannot be sold or transferred until the court resolves the underlying claim. They consume the same amount of family time, generate the same legal fees, and produce the same emotional cost as a probate proceeding would.

> **REFLECTION**
>
> When a family discovers, after a death, that a house has been pulled into court, the immediate reaction is often that someone made a mistake. Sometimes that is true. More often, the structure that produced the proceeding existed for years and was simply never addressed. The discovery is not the failure; the discovery is the revelation of a failure that happened long before.

What This Looks Like in Practice

A family — call them the Henderson family — believes their estate plan is complete. The mother, a widow, has a revocable living trust naming her three adult children as equal beneficiaries. The trust was drafted in 2009 by competent counsel. The mother's home was funded into the trust at that time. The mother's investment account, naming the three children as transfer-on-death beneficiaries, is set to pass outside probate. The mother's bank account, with one child as POD, is set to pass outside probate.

The mother dies in 2026. Within two weeks, the family discovers three problems. First, the mother bought a small lake house in another state in 2018 and never moved it into the trust — that property requires ancillary probate in the state where the lake is located. Second, the mother had refinanced her primary home in 2021 and the trust attorney's follow-up deed back into the trust was never recorded — that property requires probate in the home state. Third, the mother had been informally caring for an elderly cousin's investment property for the last three years, with the cousin paying the taxes and the mother managing the rentals; on the cousin's death six months ago, the cousin had named the mother as one of three tenants-in-common heirs — an interest the mother never had time to address before her own death, and which now requires probate in a third state.

What had appeared to be a clean, fully funded trust plan turned out to be a three-state probate problem. The aggregate cost — in legal fees, court costs, executor compensation, and family time — exceeded thirty thousand dollars. Each of the three problems was knowable during life. None had been addressed.

The Henderson story is unusual only in concentration. Most families have one of these problems. Many have two. A small minority have all three. The book's argument throughout is that none of these patterns is exotic; they are common, predictable, and largely preventable with annual review of the deeds, the trust funding, and the multi-state property roster.

Where We Go From Here

Notes on Practice

The recurring observation among practitioners who handle post-mortem real-property cases is that the family's first reaction — "somebody made a mistake" — is almost always wrong. The structural failures that pull houses into court are rarely the result of recent error. They are the result of decisions made (or not made) years or decades earlier that the family has only now been forced to examine. The mistake, if there is one, is almost always the absence of annual review — the failure to look at the deeds while they could still be corrected without consequence.

A second observation: ancillary probate is the single most expensive category of preventable post-mortem real-property expense. The economics favor planning by an order of magnitude. Any family with real property in more than one state should treat the question of multi-state titling as a high-priority matter, addressed during life rather than after death.

The Title-Chain Reconstruction Project

When a family discovers, after a death, that the recorded title chain on a particular property is broken or ambiguous, the cure is a procedure most practitioners call title-chain reconstruction. The process involves assembling every recorded instrument affecting the property — every deed, every mortgage, every release, every easement, every judgment, every probate order — from the date of the earliest defect in the chain forward to the present. Title-insurance companies maintain extensive plant records and can usually produce the documents from the past forty to sixty years for a modest fee. Older documents may require physical retrieval from the recorder's office.

Once the chain is assembled, the gap or defect is identified and a corrective instrument is drafted to cure it. Common corrective instruments include: an affidavit of heirship (when an intermediate intestate succession was never formally administered); a confirmatory deed (when a deed was prepared but never recorded, or when the recorded deed has a typographical defect); a quiet-title judgment (when the defect is contested or where the corrective parties cannot all be located); or an agreement of cotenants (when the dispute is among the current owners and they can agree on the cure).

Title-chain reconstruction is unglamorous work that can consume weeks of attorney time and several thousand dollars in fees. It is also the cure that allows the property to be sold, refinanced, or passed cleanly to the next generation. For many families, the cost is trivial relative to the value preserved.

Edge Case — The Cloud on Title from Old Mortgages

A subtle and frequent title defect: an old mortgage that was paid off but never formally released. The release deed (also called a satisfaction of mortgage or reconveyance) should have been recorded by the lender promptly after the loan payoff. If it was not, the mortgage continues to appear in the title chain as an unsatisfied lien, even though the underlying debt has been paid for years.

Cleaning up an old un-released mortgage typically requires tracking down the lender (which may have been acquired or merged), obtaining a duplicate satisfaction or release, and recording it. Where the lender no longer exists and no successor can be identified, the cure is usually a quiet-title action — an evidentiary proceeding in which the current owner shows the court that the underlying debt has been paid and seeks a court order extinguishing the recorded lien. The proceeding takes months and several thousand dollars in fees but produces a clean title that supports any future transaction.

Common Questions, Briefly

Can I avoid ancillary probate by giving someone a power of attorney over my out-of-state property?

No. A power of attorney terminates at the principal's death; it has no post-mortem effect. To avoid ancillary probate, the property itself must be titled in a way that transfers outside probate — trust ownership, joint tenancy, transfer-on-death deed, or LLC ownership. A lifetime power of attorney is irrelevant after death.

Does an LLC really avoid ancillary probate even though it owns real property?

Yes, when the structure is properly maintained. The LLC is the recorded owner of the real property in the situs state. The deceased's estate owns an LLC membership interest, which is personal property governed by the law of the deceased's domicile (not the situs state). The domiciliary probate (or trust administration, if the LLC interest is held in trust) administers the membership interest. The underlying real property does not change hands at all; the LLC continues to own it. No ancillary probate is required.

Practitioner Patterns — When Court Is Unavoidable

While most of this chapter has focused on patterns that drag properties into court that should have stayed out, it is worth acknowledging that some matters genuinely require court resolution and cannot be avoided by planning, no matter how careful. Three categories merit explicit recognition because counsel sometimes mistake them for preventable patterns.

The first is the contested capacity case. When a property owner's mental capacity at the time of a critical instrument — a deed, a trust amendment, a will — is genuinely doubtful, and when the parties affected by the instrument disagree about its validity, only the court can resolve the dispute. Mediation can sometimes settle the matter on terms the parties accept, but the underlying capacity question is fact-intensive and evidentiary, and absent settlement the only forum is the probate court. Counsel handling these cases should manage client expectations carefully: the proceedings are slow, expensive, and emotionally damaging, even where the outcome is ultimately favorable.

The second is the genuinely contested boundary or easement case. Some real properties carry historical ambiguities about their physical extent — a survey discrepancy, an unrecorded easement that has been used for decades, a fence that does not match the legal description. These ambiguities sometimes ripen into disputes when the property changes hands, and only a quiet-title action can definitively resolve them. For inheriting families, these matters are most often discovered when a buyer's title company raises an objection that requires court resolution before closing.

The third is the contested intestate succession. When a property owner dies intestate and the family disagrees about who counts as a statutory heir — competing claims of marriage, paternity, or kinship — the court is the only forum that can establish the controlling facts. These cases are uncommon but not rare; they appear most often in families where the deceased had complicated personal circumstances during life that were not fully discussed with the heirs before death. The cure during life is a valid will that names the deceased's intended beneficiaries explicitly, eliminating any need for subsequent statutory analysis.

Part V takes up the human side of the question — what disputes actually arise after death, why families fight over houses with such intensity, and what tools exist to defuse the conflict. Chapter 8 catalogs the disputes themselves. Chapter 9 explains why they are so often more painful than the underlying property is worth.

Figure 7.1

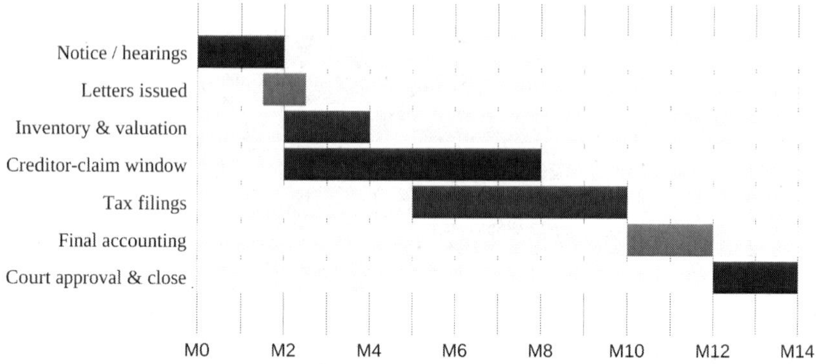

When properties get pulled into court — the recurring structural failures and where they sit on the timeline.

KEY POINT

When a family discovers, after a death, that a house has been pulled into court, the immediate reaction is often that someone made a mistake. More often, the structure that produced the proceeding existed for years and was simply never addressed. The discovery is the revelation of a failure that happened long before.

What This Chapter Has Said

Six recurring patterns account for the great majority of post-mortem real-property court proceedings: improper titling, outdated deeds, incomplete trust funding, conflicting ownership claims, multi-state property, and tort or specific-performance claims. Each is anticipatable and largely preventable with annual review of the deeds, the trust funding, and the multi-state property roster. Improper titling is the simplest pattern: the deed did not say what the family thought it said. Outdated deeds accumulate over decades — predeceased joint tenants, dissolved marriages, amended trusts. Multi-state property triggers ancillary probate unless held in trust, by transfer-on-death deed, or through an LLC. The cost of fixing these patterns during life is, in any reasonable estate, a fraction of the cost of cleaning them up afterward.

PART V

◆

THE HUMAN SIDE

Why families fight over houses, what those fights are really about, and what tools exist to defuse them.

CHAPTER 8

Common Property Disputes After Death

Chapter at a Glance

- The four questions around which co-tenant disputes typically revolve: who can live there, who pays expenses, who decides whether to sell, and who controls access.
- The default rules: a co-tenant in possession owes no rent unless ousted; co-tenants who pay more than their share have a right of contribution.
- What contribution claims are available for what categories of expense — and why documentation matters.
- The three options when co-tenants disagree about whether to sell: negotiated buyout, continued co-tenancy with later revisit, or partition.
- The right-of-first-refusal solution and the value of a written co-tenancy agreement entered into before the conflict appears.

Property disputes after death usually revolve around four questions:

- Who can live there?
- Who pays the expenses?
- Who decides whether to sell?
- Who controls access?

These disputes are rarely about law. They are about misaligned expectations. Clear ownership resolves conflict faster than negotiation does, because clear ownership makes negotiation unnecessary on the questions where the deed has already spoken.

Where the disputes are real, the courts have well-developed tools to resolve them — partition, accounting between cotenants, ejectment, and equitable contribution. Where the disputes are more about feeling than about title, the courts cannot resolve them at all; the only forum that can is the family itself.

Dispute Type One — Who Can Live There

Every co-owner of real property has the right to possess and use the entire property, subject to the equal rights of the other co-owners. This is true of joint tenants, tenants in common, tenants by the entirety, and beneficiaries of a trust (if the trust agreement so provides). The right of possession is fundamental and cannot be defeated by the wishes of one co-owner over the others.

When one co-owner is in possession of the property and the others are not, three legal questions follow:

1. **Is the occupant a tenant of the others?** Generally no, unless the co-owners have entered into an express written agreement creating a leasehold. The default rule is that a co-owner in possession owes no rent to the non-occupying co-owners.
2. **Does the occupant owe the others their share of the use value?** Generally only if the others have been ousted — that is, physically excluded from the property by the occupant's actions or threats. Mere absence is not ouster.
3. **Does the occupant owe an accounting for income generated from the property?** Yes. If the property generates rental income, royalty income, or other revenue, the occupant must account to the other co-owners for their share.

These rules are old, durable, and reasonably uniform across the states. They were developed for an agrarian economy in which a co-tenant might farm a piece of jointly held land for years without producing any conflict. They sometimes feel anomalous in modern residential settings, where a sibling living rent-free in a parents' house held by all the siblings as tenants in common produces immediate friction. The friction is real, but the friction does not change the rule.

When Ouster Occurs

Ouster — the legal concept that triggers a duty to pay rent to the other co-tenants — requires more than the occupant's quiet occupancy. It requires affirmative acts that exclude the others. Examples include changing the locks without notice, refusing access on demand, denying the others the right to enter, or openly claiming exclusive ownership. When ouster occurs, the ousted co-tenants may recover their fair share of the property's rental value from the date of ouster forward.

Most family situations do not involve ouster, even when the non-occupants feel excluded. The sibling who has lived in the parents' house for fifteen years and who, after the parents' death, continues to live there without paying rent to the other siblings is often acting within the legal default. The other siblings' option, if they want a different arrangement, is to negotiate a written occupancy agreement, demand partition, or treat the matter as part of broader settlement discussions about the entire estate.

Dispute Type Two — Who Pays the Expenses

Real property generates ongoing expenses — property taxes, homeowners' insurance, utilities, mortgage payments, maintenance, and capital improvements. A co-owner who pays more than their proportional share has a right of contribution against the other co-owners for the excess.

The right of contribution is well-established but unevenly enforced in practice. The contributing co-owner often does not press the right because the other co-owners are family members, the amounts seem small in any given month, and the prospect of demanding repayment from a sibling feels ungenerous. By the time the matter ripens — often during partition or sale — the claimed contribution has accumulated to a substantial sum, and the other co-owners dispute its computation, its necessity, or its supporting documentation.

Three categories of expense are worth distinguishing:

Table 8.1

Expense category	Contribution available	Notes
Property taxes	Yes — proportional	Universally recognized; documented through receipts.
Mortgage principal & interest	Yes — proportional	Where the loan was joint or assumed by all co-tenants.
Hazard insurance	Yes — proportional	Standard maintenance of the asset; recoverable.
Necessary repairs (roof, plumbing, structural)	Yes — proportional	Recoverable; documented through receipts.
Capital improvements (additions, kitchen)	Limited	Recoverable to the extent of value added at sale.
Utilities (occupant uses)	Generally no	Treated as cost of occupant's possession.
Discretionary cosmetic upgrades	Generally no	Not necessary to preserve the asset; not recoverable.
Property-management fees (when self-managed)	Limited	Not recoverable in most jurisdictions; some states allow.

Co-tenant contribution rights for common categories of property expense.

Contribution claims are accountable in partition or in a separate action between co-tenants. The complexity of the accounting is one reason partition actions take as long as they do; many cases involve fifteen to twenty years of receipts to be reviewed.

Dispute Type Three — Who Decides Whether to Sell

This is the hardest of the four. There is no provision of American property law that requires co-tenants to agree on whether to sell. There is no majority rule, no buyout right at fair value, no court-supervised vote — except in the partition proceeding itself, where the court can order a sale that no co-tenant wanted but at least one demanded.

When co-tenants disagree about whether to sell, three paths are available:

1. **Negotiate a buyout.** The co-tenant who wants to sell offers their share to the co-tenant who wants to keep the property at an agreed valuation. The simplest and least costly resolution; requires both parties' willingness.
2. **Continue the co-tenancy and revisit later.** Sometimes the right answer is to do nothing for a year, let the immediate emotional pressure subside, and revisit the question. The property is patient; the co-owners may not be.
3. **Petition for partition.** The remedy of last resort. Any co-tenant can compel a sale or division through partition. The proceeding is slow, expensive, and often produces a sale at a price below market — but it does, eventually, end the disagreement.

The Right of First Refusal Solution

Many sophisticated co-tenancy arrangements include a contractual right of first refusal — a provision that, before any co-tenant can sell to a third party, that co-tenant must first offer the share to the other co-tenants at the same price. The right of first refusal preserves the property within the family while allowing each co-tenant to exit when they wish.

Where a tenancy-in-common arose by inheritance and no such contractual right exists, the family can create one after the fact by entering into a written co-tenancy agreement. The agreement is binding on the parties who sign it; it does not bind future inheritors of any co-tenant's share unless the agreement is recorded and runs with the land. Counsel can draft such an agreement in a few hours of work.

Dispute Type Four — Who Controls Access

The fourth category of dispute is the most petty and the most frequent. Who has the keys? Who is allowed to enter? Who can bring a guest? Who controls the alarm code, the garage opener, the password to the smart-home system?

Legally, every co-owner has equal access to the entire property. Practically, one co-owner is often in possession, controls the security infrastructure, and effectively determines who else can enter. The disparity becomes a source of conflict almost immediately.

The legal remedy is a demand for access, which the occupant must honor. Refusal to honor it constitutes ouster, with the consequences described above. Most disputes do not reach this point; the parties either negotiate an arrangement (specific visit days, agreed key holders, schedule for repairs and improvements) or escalate to broader sale or partition discussions.

> **KEY POINT**
>
> Co-tenants disputes are governed by a small set of legal rules — the rights of possession, contribution, ouster, and partition — that have been settled for centuries. The underlying disputes, however, are almost always about expectations the parties never wrote down. The cure for most of them is a brief written co-tenancy agreement entered into before the conflict appears.

The Co-Tenancy Agreement

A co-tenancy agreement is a written contract among the co-owners of real property addressing the four dispute categories: occupancy, expense allocation, decision-making (including sale), and access. It can be entered into at any time during the co-tenancy and binds the parties who sign it.

A well-drafted agreement typically addresses:

- Occupancy rights and the terms (if any) under which a co-tenant in possession will pay rent to the others.
- Allocation of recurring expenses (taxes, insurance, mortgage, maintenance) and the procedure for handling extraordinary expenses (capital improvements, major

repairs).

- Decision-making procedures — who can authorize what, what requires unanimity, what requires majority, and how disputes are resolved.
- Sale procedures — including any right of first refusal, any agreed-upon valuation method, and any required notice periods.
- Termination of the agreement and conversion to alternative ownership structure (LLC, trust) if circumstances change.
- Mediation or arbitration provisions to resolve disputes without resort to court.

The agreement is not a substitute for clean titling — co-tenants who are siblings sharing an inherited home would still benefit from converting the holding to an LLC, a trust, or a more structured form — but it is a meaningful intermediate step. It captures the parties' expectations while they are still reasonable and produces enforceable consequences when one party later wishes to behave otherwise.

What This Looks Like in Practice

Three siblings — call them Adam, Beth, and Carla — inherited their parents' home as tenants in common, equally, when their mother died. Adam, who was the principal caregiver during their mother's last illness, had been living in the home for the previous four years. Beth lives in another state and visited twice a year. Carla lives within an hour and visited monthly.

In the first six months after the death, the siblings did not address the property. Adam continued to live there, paid the property taxes and the utilities, and made minor repairs. Beth and Carla, in conversation, both assumed the long-term plan was to sell the house and divide the proceeds equally.

At the one-year mark, Beth raised the question. Adam — who had by now invested four thousand dollars in repairs and another two thousand in property taxes — said he wanted to buy his siblings' shares and continue living there. Carla agreed in principle but at a price ten percent above what Adam was offering. Beth wanted simply to sell on the open market and divide the proceeds three ways.

Eighteen months after the death, the disagreement was still unresolved. Adam was now claiming a contribution credit for his accumulated expenses; Beth was challenging some of the expenses as cosmetic; Carla had hired her own attorney. By the twenty-fourth month, Beth filed a petition for partition. The case took an additional twenty months to conclude. The court ordered a sale at public auction, which produced a price approximately twelve percent below what an open-market sale would have produced eighteen months earlier. Attorneys' fees consumed approximately fifteen thousand dollars of the proceeds. Adam's contribution claim was partially recognized but reduced for the items Beth had successfully challenged.

All three siblings ended up with less money than any of them would have received from a negotiated buyout in month nine, and none of them remained on speaking terms by the time the matter closed. The arithmetic of the partition was the easy part; the family relationships were the part that the proceeding could not repair.

Where We Go From Here

Notes on Practice

Two practical observations recur in co-tenant disputes. First, the contribution accounting is almost always the hardest part of any partition or buyout settlement. Co-tenants who paid more than their share of expenses rarely kept contemporaneous records; co-tenants who paid nothing rarely accept the others' reconstructions. The single most useful intervention is contemporaneous documentation: every co-tenant who pays property expenses should record the payment in a shared spreadsheet, with the receipt scanned and saved, every month. The documentation costs minutes per month and eliminates years of subsequent dispute.

Second, the right of first refusal in a written co-tenancy agreement is one of the most underutilized tools in the field. Where co-tenants want to preserve the property within the family while allowing each co-owner to exit when they wish, the right of first refusal accomplishes both objectives. The documents to create one are simple. The cost is modest. The reduction in subsequent dispute risk is substantial.

Drafting a Co-Tenancy Agreement — Specific Provisions

A useful co-tenancy agreement runs five to fifteen pages and addresses, at minimum, the following ten topics:

1. **Identification of co-tenants and respective interests.** Names, addresses, fractional interests, and source of ownership (inheritance, purchase, gift).

2. **Property identification.** Legal description, parcel number, recording reference, and physical address.

3. **Occupancy and use.** Who may occupy, on what schedule, and on what terms. Whether occupancy is rotating, permanent, or by agreement.

4. **Allocation of recurring expenses.** Property tax, insurance, mortgage, HOA dues, utilities. Proportional or fixed-amount; payment schedule and reimbursement procedure.

5. **Major repairs and capital improvements.** Threshold above which co-tenant consent is required; approval procedure; recovery upon sale.

6. **Decision-making procedures.** Unanimous, majority, or weighted by interest; what decisions require what level of consent.

7. **Right of first refusal.** Procedure for offering an interest to other co-tenants before sale to a third party; valuation method; response window.

8. **Sale procedures.** How a sale is initiated, how the price is determined, how proceeds are distributed.

9. **Dispute resolution.** Mediation, arbitration, or judicial process; governing-law and venue selection.

10. **Termination and successor co-tenants.** How the agreement terminates; how it binds (or does not bind) successors-in-interest; whether to record as a covenant running with the land.

Local counsel can produce such an agreement in a few billable hours. The agreement does not need to be perfect — the act of drafting it usually surfaces and resolves differences in expectation that would otherwise have ripened into litigation. Many co-tenant relationships stabilize for years simply because the parties have one honest conversation about the topics above.

When Mediation Works (and When It Does Not)

Mediation — facilitated negotiation among the co-tenants with a neutral third party — works in approximately two-thirds of co-tenant disputes that reach it. Mediation succeeds when (a) all co-tenants have a long-term interest in maintaining family relationships, (b) the underlying disagreement is about valuation or process rather than core entitlement, and (c) the parties are willing to make compromises that fall within a reasonable range of the eventual judicial outcome.

Mediation does not work — and is sometimes a costly delay — when (a) one party has decided that the family relationship is no longer worth preserving, (b) the underlying disagreement is about the validity of ownership itself (a will contest, an undue-influence claim against the grantor of a critical deed), or (c) one party has pursued litigation aggressively enough that the other party feels coerced into mediating from a weakened position. In these cases, the dispute typically must run through formal adjudication before resolution is possible. Counsel should evaluate honestly which category a particular case falls into before recommending (or scheduling) mediation.

Common Questions, Briefly

If I'm a co-tenant who wants to keep the house, how do I value it for a buyout?

The most defensible valuation method is two independent appraisals — one selected by the buyout proposer, one by the recipient — with the agreed buyout price set at the average of the two. A single jointly selected appraiser also works. Negotiated valuations based on online estimates (Zillow, Redfin) are unreliable and frequently produce disputes; pay for the formal appraisals.

Can I rent out the property over my co-tenants' objections?

You can lease your own fractional interest, but the lease binds only your interest. The lessee takes a fractional right of possession subject to the equal rights of the other co-tenants. As a practical matter, this is rarely useful (no commercial tenant will accept a fractional lease), so the result is functional deadlock. The cure is consensus among all co-tenants or, ultimately, partition.

Practitioner Patterns — When Buyouts Work

The negotiated buyout — one co-tenant purchases the interests of the others at an agreed price — is the most successful resolution path for inherited co-tenancy disputes. It preserves the property within the family, honors the desire of the most-attached heir to continue the connection, and gives the less-attached heirs liquidity. But buyouts succeed only under specific conditions, and counsel evaluating a particular case should assess these conditions honestly before recommending the buyout path.

First, the buyout requires that one co-tenant has the financial capacity to purchase the others' shares. For modest-value properties this is usually achievable; for high-value urban properties it can be prohibitive. Where the buying co-tenant lacks immediate cash, structured installment sales (with the property serving as security) can bridge the gap, but the financing arrangement introduces its own complexity and counterparty risk. The buyout works best when the buying co-tenant can fund the purchase outright or with conventional financing.

Second, the buyout requires agreed valuation. The most successful approach uses two independent appraisals — one selected by the buyer, one by the sellers — with the buyout price set at the average. This avoids the asymmetric incentives that destroy informal valuation discussions: the buyer wants a low price, the sellers want a high price, and neither party trusts the other's characterization of the market. Two appraisals objectively performed and arithmetically averaged is a process that all parties can accept as fair.

Third, the buyout requires that the parties want it to succeed. Where one party has decided that the family relationship is no longer worth preserving, no buyout structure will produce agreement; the matter must run through partition. Counsel evaluating a case for buyout viability should listen carefully to what each party is actually saying about the others. The buyout is for families that still see themselves as families. For families that no longer do, the partition is the cleaner path forward, however regrettable.

Where the conditions are met, the buyout typically completes within sixty to ninety days from agreement on appraisal method to recorded transfer. Cost is modest — two appraisals at $500–$1,000 each, attorney fees of $2,000 to $5,000, recording fees of a few hundred dollars. The total is usually less than ten thousand dollars — perhaps one to three percent of the property value — compared to fifteen to thirty percent for a contested partition. The economics, like the relationships, favor the buyout where it is achievable.

Chapter 9 takes up the deeper question — why families fight over houses with the intensity that they do, even when the underlying property is not the most valuable thing in the estate. The reasons are partly economic and largely emotional, and they have specific structural causes that are worth naming.

Figure 8.1

TEN ELEMENTS OF A USEFUL CO-TENANCY AGREEMENT

1. Co-tenants & shares
2. Property identification
3. Occupancy & use
4. Recurring expense allocation
5. Major repairs & improvements
6. Decision-making procedures
7. Right of first refusal
8. Sale procedures
9. Dispute resolution
10. Termination & successors

The ten elements of a useful co-tenancy agreement — drafted before the conflict, not after.

KEY POINT

Co-tenant disputes are governed by a small set of legal rules — possession, contribution, ouster, partition — that have been settled for centuries. The underlying disputes are almost always about expectations the parties never wrote down. The cure for most of them is a brief written co-tenancy agreement entered into before the conflict appears.

What This Chapter Has Said

Co-tenant disputes typically revolve around four questions: who can live there, who pays expenses, who decides whether to sell, and who controls access. The default rules are settled but rarely match the family's expectations. A co-tenant in possession owes no rent unless ousted. A co-tenant who pays more than their share of necessary expenses has a right of contribution. No co-tenant can be forced to agree on sale; partition is the remedy of last resort and is always available. The cure for most disputes is a written co-tenancy agreement that addresses occupancy, expenses, decision-making, sale procedures, and exit mechanics. Drafted before the conflict, the agreement captures expectations while they are still reasonable. Drafted after the conflict, the agreement is rarely achievable.

CHAPTER 9

Why Families Fight Over Houses

Chapter at a Glance

- Why the family home represents stability, memory, and perceived fairness in ways that other inherited assets do not.
- The five recurring conflict patterns: the unequal inheritor, the blended-family second-marriage outcome, the sibling who lived there, investor co-owners turned sentimental co-owners, and the property nobody wants.
- Why the legal system can resolve the technical questions but cannot resolve the underlying emotional ones.
- Five tools that defuse the great majority of post-mortem property conflicts before they escalate into litigation.
- Five responses that families instinctively try and that consistently fail.

Houses represent stability, memory, and perceived fairness. When ownership outcomes differ from emotional expectations, conflict escalates. Understanding the legal outcome early — what the deed actually says, what each ownership form actually produces — often prevents unnecessary escalation later. But even with perfect understanding, some families fight, and those fights are worth understanding on their own terms.

What the House Represents

For most American families, the family home is more than the largest asset on the balance sheet. It is the physical container of decades of family history. It is the room where the children grew up, the kitchen where the holidays were celebrated, the back yard where the dog is buried, the dining-room table that has hosted a thousand difficult conversations. The asset value of the house is a number on a tax assessment. The meaning of the house is something else.

When a parent dies, the house becomes a stand-in for the parent. Decisions about the house are heard, by the family, as decisions about the parent's memory. Selling the house feels like erasing the parent. Keeping the house feels like preserving them. Neither response is irrational. Both are complicated by the fact that the legal system treats the house as a piece of property and the family treats it as a biographical artifact.

Three particular features of the family home make it more conflict-prone than other inherited assets:

1. **It is unique.** Unlike a stock portfolio or a bank account, a house cannot be divided proportionally without destroying its value. The family that inherits a million-dollar brokerage account can split it down the middle in fifteen minutes. The family that inherits a million-dollar house cannot.

2. **It carries memory.** Each family member's relationship to the house is private and personal. The sibling who has not visited in a decade may still feel a deep attachment to the house's existence. The sibling who lived there as a caregiver may feel an even deeper one. These attachments do not aggregate into a shared family view; they conflict.

3. **It is visible.** Decisions about the house are public to the extended family. Who got the house. Who is living in it. Who agreed to its sale. These decisions are visible to extended family in ways that the disposition of a brokerage account is not. The visibility raises the stakes and prolongs the dispute.

The Five Recurring Conflict Patterns

Five conflict patterns arise repeatedly in post-mortem real-property practice. Each has its own dynamic, its own tells, and its own customary resolution path.

(1) The unequal inheritor. One child receives the house — by joint titling, by transfer-on-death deed, by trust direction, or by will — while the other children receive cash equivalents of lesser value. The disparity may have reflected the parent's deliberate decision (to compensate the child who provided care, to recognize a previous gift to one of the others, to disinherit a child the parent had estranged from). It may have reflected an accident of titling that the parent did not understand. The other

children, in either case, often experience the disparity as unfair. The conflict that follows is rarely about the asset value alone; it is about the perceived favoritism the disposition appears to encode.

(2) The blended-family second-marriage outcome. The deceased's second spouse inherits the marital home — by survivorship, by will, or by elective share — and the deceased's children from the prior marriage receive nothing or only a residual interest. The children often believe (sometimes correctly, sometimes not) that the deceased intended a more balanced outcome and that the second spouse's effective inheritance of the home was an unintended consequence of incomplete planning. The conflict that follows can stretch for years and frequently outlasts the second spouse's own death, when the children of the prior marriage discover that the second spouse has left the home to the second spouse's children, completing the disinheritance.

(3) The sibling who lived there. The adult child who lived in the parents' house for years before the parents' death — often as a caregiver — wants to continue living there after the death. The other siblings, who jointly inherited the house, want their share of the value. The negotiation is awkward because the sibling in possession has both a strong attachment to the property and a real economic incentive to minimize their valuation of it. The other siblings have the opposite economic incentive. The matter

is rarely resolved on the merits of the property's value; it is resolved on the weight of the sibling relationships.

(4) The investor co-owners who became sentimental co-owners. Three friends bought a vacation property together as tenants in common, intending to use it for ten years and then sell. Twenty years later, two of the three friends have died and the property is now owned by the third surviving friend, two spouses of the deceased friends, four adult children of the deceased friends, and a niece of one. The property has become the centerpiece of family vacations for the surviving investors' children, who have no business or financial relationship to one another and have widely varying views about whether and how to continue the arrangement. What had been a three-way investment partnership is now an eight-way emotional negotiation.

(5) The property nobody wants. The family inherits a piece of property — a remote piece of farmland, a deteriorating vacation cabin, a commercial property in a declining town — that none of the inheritors actually wants. Each is reluctant to take ownership (because of expense, distance, or hassle); each is reluctant to sell at the offered prices (because of sentimental attachment or unrealistic price expectation). The property accumulates expenses, depreciates, and becomes a chronic source of irritation. Years pass. Nothing is done.

Why the Legal System Cannot Resolve These Conflicts

The legal system has well-developed tools for the legal questions: it can determine title, allocate contribution, order partition, confirm distributions. It has nothing to offer for the underlying emotional questions: who the parent loved most, who deserves what, what the family's history is supposed to mean.

The mismatch between what the legal system can address and what the family is actually fighting about is the source of most of the dissatisfaction families report with post-mortem property litigation. The court answers the technical question. The family is left with the emotional question untouched. Often the court's answer to the technical question makes the emotional question harder, because the resolution of the technical question requires the family to act in ways that imply, however falsely, an answer to the emotional one.

REFLECTION

Most family disputes over inherited property are not really disputes about the property. They are disputes about the relationship between the inheritors, conducted through the property because the property is the only object that everyone can see at once. Resolving the property question rarely resolves the underlying relationship question. The relationship question must be resolved on its own terms, by the people involved, with or without the help of mediation or counseling.

What Tools Exist to Defuse the Conflict

Five tools, used in combination, defuse the great majority of post-mortem property conflicts before they escalate into litigation.

(1) The pre-death conversation. The single most effective intervention is a conversation before the death — among the parents and the adult children — about what the parents intend and why. The conversation is uncomfortable; it is often the most uncomfortable conversation the family will ever have. It is also the conversation that prevents most of what comes after. Adult children who learn, during the parents' lifetimes, that the family home will pass to one sibling and not to the others — and who hear the parents explain why — almost never litigate that disposition after death. Children who learn the outcome by reading a will for the first time at the funeral very often do.

(2) The professionally drafted estate plan. The family that engages an estate-planning attorney to think through the real-property dispositions in advance — and that funds the trust properly, retitles the deeds appropriately, and signs a transfer-on-death instrument where useful — eliminates the great majority of post-mortem surprises. The cost of doing this work during life is, in any reasonable estate, a fraction of the cost of cleaning it up after death.

(3) The buyout option, structured in advance. Where multiple children will inherit a property and one is likely to want to buy

out the others, the trust agreement or letter of instruction can pre-specify a valuation method (qualified appraiser, average of two appraisals) and a payment schedule (immediate cash, five-year installment with interest). Pre-specification eliminates the negotiation in which the occupant and the non-occupants have opposite economic incentives and converts the question into a simple computational exercise.

(4) The family meeting and the third-party facilitator. Where multiple inheritors must collectively decide the future of a property, a single facilitated meeting — with an attorney, a family-law mediator, or a financial-planning professional — produces a far higher rate of agreement than open-ended informal discussion. The facilitator's role is to keep the conversation focused on the technical questions (valuation, occupancy terms, expense allocation) rather than the emotional ones (favoritism, history, perceived slights).

(5) The structured exit mechanism. Even after the property has been inherited, the co-owners can convert the holding to a more structured arrangement — an LLC with operating agreement, a trust with explicit distribution rules, a written co-tenancy agreement with right of first refusal. Each of these adds internal procedure to the co-ownership and substantially reduces the probability that the co-owners will end up in partition court.

What Doesn't Defuse the Conflict

It is also worth naming the responses that families instinctively try and that consistently fail.

- Avoiding the conversation. Pretending the property issue does not exist, on the theory that time will resolve it, almost always makes the conflict worse. The expenses accumulate. The resentment compounds. The eventual confrontation is harder than the early one would have been.
- Trying to be fair through informal arrangements. Verbal promises about future buyouts, handshake deals about expense allocation, and family-meeting consensus that no one writes down all dissolve under the first stress. Anything material should be in writing.
- Letting the sibling who lived there decide. The sibling in possession has both information advantage and emotional standing the others do not have. The decision-making weight should be balanced procedurally — a facilitated meeting, an independent appraisal — not by deferring to the sibling who happens to be on the property.
- Using the property as currency in unrelated family negotiations. ("If you let me keep the house, I won't contest the will.") These quid pro quo arrangements rarely hold up over time and frequently reopen years later when one party perceives the original deal as having been unequal.

- Hiring lawyers immediately. Lawyers are necessary at certain points (drafting agreements, conducting partition if it becomes necessary) but their early arrival often hardens positions that could have been negotiated less expensively in a different posture.

What This Looks Like in Practice

Two siblings — call them Diana and Eric — lose their mother at age eighty-three. The mother's estate consists primarily of the family home in California, valued at approximately one million two hundred thousand dollars, with a mortgage of about ninety thousand dollars remaining. The mother's revocable trust leaves the home in equal shares to Diana and Eric. The trust is properly funded; no probate is required.

Diana lives within an hour of the home and visited her mother weekly during the mother's last years. Eric lives across the country and visited twice a year. Both are in their late fifties. Both are financially comfortable. Both loved the mother.

In the third week after the death, Diana and Eric have lunch. Diana tells Eric that she would like to buy his half of the house and live in it; she had been planning to retire in California anyway. Eric is initially supportive but uneasy about the valuation. Diana suggests an appraisal. Eric suggests two appraisals — one of his choosing, one of Diana's — with the average to control the buyout price.

The two appraisals come in at one million one hundred fifty thousand and one million two hundred sixty thousand. The average is one million two hundred five thousand. Less the mortgage of ninety thousand, the equity is approximately one million one hundred fifteen thousand. Diana owes Eric half — approximately five hundred fifty-eight thousand.

Diana does not have that amount in cash. Eric proposes a five-year installment with interest at the prime rate plus one percent, secured by a recorded second deed of trust against the property. Diana agrees. Their attorney drafts the documents in two weeks. Eric receives a payment that funds his retirement plans. Diana retitles the property into her own name and moves in within three months of the death.

The siblings remain on excellent terms throughout the process. Their children speak about it later as the moment they understood that the parents had raised them, in a quiet way, to be the kind of adults who could navigate this particular transition without breaking the family.

The Diana-and-Eric outcome is achievable. It is not automatic. It requires that the parties enter the conversation with goodwill, that they use a facilitative process (the two-appraisal valuation method) rather than a negotiation in which their opposing economic interests dominate, and that they translate their agreement promptly into recorded documents. None of these steps is mysterious. All of them require, primarily, the will to do the work.

Where We Go From Here

Notes on Practice

The single most powerful intervention against family conflict over inherited property is also the simplest: a single conversation, held before the parents die, in which the parents tell the adult children what they intend and why. The conversation is uncomfortable. It is frequently the most uncomfortable conversation the family ever has. It is also the conversation that prevents almost all of the litigation.

Adult children who learn during the parents' lifetimes that the family home will pass in a particular way — and who hear the parents explain the reasoning — almost never litigate that disposition after death. Children who learn the disposition for the first time at the funeral very often do. The variable is not the disposition itself. The variable is whether the children had the chance to absorb it while the parents were still available to explain it.

The Family Meeting — A Practical Framework

When the family decides to hold a meeting to discuss inherited property, the structure of the meeting matters more than the content. A poorly structured meeting compounds existing tensions. A well-structured meeting produces resolution even on emotionally complex issues.

Five elements characterize a productive family meeting:

1. **A neutral facilitator.** Ideally a family-business consultant, a mediator, or an estate-planning attorney with mediation training. The facilitator's role is to keep the conversation focused, give every participant equal time, and translate emotional language into procedural language. A family member cannot perform this role; the appearance of neutrality is essential.

2. **A defined agenda, distributed in advance.** Every participant should know what topics will be discussed and what decisions are sought. Surprises produce defensive reactions. Predictability produces engagement.

3. **A neutral location.** Not the property in question, not any participant's home, not any participant's place of business. A conference room at a professional office is ideal. Neutrality of setting reduces territoriality.

4. **A defined time limit.** Two to four hours is appropriate for most meetings. Longer meetings produce fatigue and defensive decision-making. If the work is not complete in the scheduled time, schedule a follow-up rather than extending the current session.

5. **Written outcomes.** Whatever is decided in the meeting should be reduced to writing the same day, distributed to all participants for review, and confirmed within a week. Verbal agreements that are not promptly memorialized

almost always disintegrate within thirty days.

Families who follow this framework report substantially higher rates of post-meeting agreement than families who approach the conversation informally. The framework does not guarantee agreement — some disputes are too far gone for any process to repair — but it dramatically improves the odds for the cases that have any prospect of resolution at all.

When the Conflict Cannot Be Resolved

It is worth acknowledging directly that some family disputes over inherited property cannot be resolved by any framework, any facilitator, or any amount of patient negotiation. The relationships are too damaged. The interests are too divergent. The history is too long. In these cases, the partition action is not a failure; it is the recognized mechanism by which the law allows co-tenants to end an arrangement they no longer wish to continue.

Counsel and family advisors do their clients a disservice when they push toward continued co-tenancy in cases where the relationships are clearly broken. The honest counsel explains the partition option, describes its costs and timeline candidly, and lets the client decide whether the alternative — continued deadlock with progressively deteriorating relationships — is preferable. Often it is not. Partition, for all its expense and its emotional cost, is sometimes the cleanest available exit.

Common Questions, Briefly

How do I tell my siblings that the parents left the house to me alone?

Tell them directly, in person, before the funeral if possible — and tell them why, to the extent the parents shared the reasoning. Do not let them learn from the will reading or from a lawyer's letter. The directness will be uncomfortable in the moment and will be the single most important thing you can do to preserve the relationships. Indirect disclosure produces lasting resentment; direct disclosure produces short-term pain that the family can move through.

Should I offer my siblings money out of my own pocket to make the inheritance more equal?

Sometimes — but consult counsel first. Voluntary post-death equalization payments are a common and generous response, but they have tax consequences (potential gift-tax filings) and can complicate the estate accounting. A coordinated equalization structured through the estate's distribution (or, where available, through qualified disclaimers within the statutory window) is usually more efficient than ad-hoc personal payments. A short consultation with the estate's attorney before proceeding is well worth the modest fee.

Practitioner Patterns — The Long Shadow of the Funeral

Family practitioners have long observed that the trajectory of post-mortem property disputes is often set in the first week — sometimes in the first hour — after the death. The decisions made during that initial period, the words spoken, the gestures made or omitted, shape what follows for months and sometimes years. Three patterns merit explicit attention because they appear with depressing regularity.

The first is the early-arrival pattern. The adult child who arrives at the parents' home within hours of the death — to attend to immediate practical matters, to be with the surviving parent, to help with funeral arrangements — frequently begins, in those first hours, to make decisions about the property that the other siblings will later question. Some of those decisions are necessary (locking up valuables, securing the residence, managing pets). Some are not. Where the early-arriving sibling makes any decision that touches property — moving items, granting access, contacting professionals — that sibling should communicate the decision immediately and explicitly to the other siblings, and should preserve all original documents and arrangements until the others can participate. The opposite pattern — early-arriving sibling makes decisions, others learn about them later — is the single most common origin story for years of subsequent intra-family conflict.

The second is the funeral-week conversation pattern. The siblings who use the funeral week to discuss substantive questions about the property — what to do with the house, who pays for what going forward, when to engage counsel — almost always do so in moments of emotional exhaustion, family stress, and incomplete information. Decisions made in that posture are rarely good ones, and they create commitments that become difficult to revise without appearing to break trust. Counsel advising families during this period should encourage explicit deferral: the property questions can wait two or three weeks until the family has had time to grieve and to gather facts. Nothing requires resolution during the funeral week. Almost everything is better resolved afterward.

The third is the executor-as-judge pattern. The named executor sometimes interprets their role as one of deciding among the family's competing claims and preferences — choosing whose interests to favor, settling family disputes about who deserves what. This interpretation is wrong as a matter of fiduciary law and wrong as a practical matter; the executor's job is to follow the will and to administer the estate per the law, not to function as a family adjudicator. The executor who presents themselves as a procedural neutral — following the instruments, applying the rules, documenting decisions — preserves family relationships to a substantially higher degree than the executor who appears to take sides. The role is hard. The discipline of neutrality is harder. Both are essential.

Part VI takes up the question of how property ownership finally resolves — what closing looks like, what life is like afterward, and why the institution of property law, taken as a whole, is what it is.

Figure 9.1

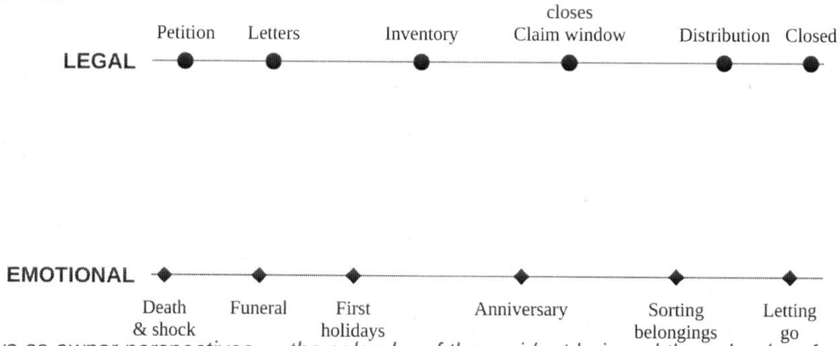

Two co-owner perspectives — the calendar of the resident heir and the calendar of the non-resident heir often diverge.

> **KEY POINT**
>
> Most family disputes over inherited property are not really disputes about the property. They are disputes about the relationship between the inheritors, conducted through the property because the property is the only object that everyone can see at once. Resolving the property question rarely resolves the underlying relationship question. The relationship question must be resolved on its own terms, by the people involved.

What This Chapter Has Said

Houses represent stability, memory, and perceived fairness in ways that other inherited assets do not. Five recurring conflict patterns — the unequal inheritor, the blended-family second-marriage outcome, the sibling who lived there, the investor co-owners turned sentimental co-owners, and the property nobody wants — produce most of the post-mortem real-property disputes in American practice. The legal system can resolve the technical questions of title and contribution but cannot resolve the emotional questions of family history and perceived favoritism. Five tools defuse most conflicts before they escalate: the pre-death conversation, the professionally drafted estate plan, the buyout option structured in advance, the family meeting with a third-party facilitator, and the structured exit mechanism. Five responses families instinctively try and that consistently fail include avoiding the conversation, relying on informal arrangements, deferring to the sibling in possession, using the property as currency in unrelated negotiations, and hiring lawyers immediately.

PART VI

◆

RESOLUTION

How property ownership finally resolves — and what life looks like once it has.

CHAPTER 10

How Property Ownership Finally Resolves

Chapter at a Glance

- The three conditions that signal final resolution: title transferred, court authority ended, trust administration stabilized.
- The three resolution pathways and the recorded instruments that complete each.
- What every new owner should receive and retain in a permanent file: certified recorded instrument, current title insurance, current property-tax statement, updated insurance policies, and complete title-chain summary.
- What survives the resolution: mortgages, property taxes, and recorded encumbrances all continue against the property in the new owner's hands.
- The income-tax consequences of resolution — particularly the basis step-up under IRC §1014 — and why a date-of-death appraisal matters for years to come.
- Why the resolution is quiet by design, and what life looks like once it is complete.

Property ownership resolves when three conditions are met:

- title is legally transferred (recorded in the new owner's name),
- court authority ends (any pending probate or partition is closed),
- trust administration stabilizes (any successor trusteeship has accepted the role and assumed responsibility).

Once these conditions are satisfied, everything else becomes easier:

- sales (the new owner can list, negotiate, and close on a clean title);
- refinancing (the lender's underwriting can proceed against an unambiguous record owner);
- occupancy decisions (the new owner can decide who lives there and on what terms);
- division of proceeds (any agreed sale yields a distributable amount to known persons).

Clarity reduces conflict. Ambiguity invites it.

The Three Resolution Pathways

Real property after death resolves along one of three pathways — each corresponding to one of the three transfer paths described in Chapter 6.

(1) Automatic resolution. Property held in joint tenancy with right of survivorship, tenancy by the entirety, community property with right of survivorship, transfer-on-death deed, Lady-Bird deed, or life estate resolves automatically at death. The recording of the death certificate (and the applicable affidavit, where required) updates the public record. The new owner appears on the next title search. The mortgage lender, the property-tax authority, the insurance carrier, and the homeowners' association recognize the new owner immediately. The full process takes a few weeks and a few hundred dollars in recording fees.

(2) Trust resolution. Property held in trust resolves when the successor trustee distributes the property out of the trust to the named beneficiary by trustee's deed, or sells the property and distributes the proceeds. The trustee has wide latitude in the timing of distribution, subject to the trust agreement and applicable trust-administration statute. In an uncomplicated case, the distribution can occur within three to six months of death. In a more complicated case (multiple beneficiaries, outstanding creditor concerns, tax filings to complete), it can take twelve to eighteen months. The proceeding is private and does not require court involvement.

(3) Probate resolution. Property held individually or as a tenant in common resolves when the probate court approves the executor's final accounting, orders the distribution to the

beneficiaries, and an executor's deed is recorded transferring title. In an uncontested case of ordinary complexity, the full proceeding takes eight to twelve months from the date of death. In a contested case, two to four years. The proceeding is public and is supervised by the probate court throughout.

The Sequence of Recording

In every pathway, the resolution culminates in a recorded instrument that updates the public record. The instrument varies by pathway.

Table 10.1

Pathway	Recorded instrument	Filed by
Joint tenancy / TBE / CPWROS	Affidavit of death of joint tenant + death certificate	Surviving co-tenant or counsel
Transfer-on-death deed	Affidavit of death and acceptance + death certificate	Beneficiary or counsel
Lady-Bird deed	Death certificate (and acceptance, if required by state)	Remainderman or counsel
Life estate	Death certificate (life estate ends automatically)	Remainderman or counsel
Trust transfer to beneficiary	Trustee's deed from trust to beneficiary	Successor trustee
Probate transfer (sale)	Court order confirming sale + executor's deed to buyer	Executor with court approval
Probate transfer (distribution in kind)	Court order of distribution + executor's deed to beneficiary	Executor with court approval

The recorded instruments that complete post-mortem property resolution.

After the recording, the new owner is the recorded owner. The title search reflects the change. Subsequent transactions (sale, refinance, encumbrance) proceed against the new owner's name. The deceased's name no longer appears in the active title chain. The property's chain of title has incorporated the death and moved on.

What Every New Owner Should Receive

At the conclusion of any of the three pathways, the new owner should receive — and should retain in a permanent file — the following five documents:

1. **A certified copy of the recorded instrument that vested title.** The affidavit of death, the trustee's deed, or the executor's deed, with the recorder's stamp showing book and page (or instrument number) and date of recording.

2. **A current title-insurance policy.** Issued in the new owner's name as of the recording date, insuring against defects of title. The cost is modest relative to the protection.

3. **A current property-tax statement.** Reissued in the new owner's name, confirming that the tax authority recognizes the change. Any past-due taxes should be addressed at this point.

4. **Updated insurance policies.** Hazard insurance and (where applicable) flood insurance transferred to the new owner. The deceased's policy is no longer adequate;

coverage gaps in the post-death window are a common but easily prevented exposure.

5. **A complete title-chain summary.** Prepared by the title company or counsel, showing every recorded instrument from the deceased's original acquisition through the current vesting. The summary is useful for any future sale or refinance and for any subsequent estate planning.

These documents are easy to obtain at the moment of resolution and substantially harder to assemble years later. The sixty minutes spent collecting them now saves many hours of stress the next time a transaction is contemplated.

What Survives the Resolution

The resolution of post-mortem property ownership ends most obligations attached to the deceased's ownership but not all. Three categories of obligation typically survive:

(1) The mortgage. The deceased's mortgage does not extinguish at death. It continues to encumber the property in the new owner's hands. The new owner is generally entitled to assume the existing mortgage under the Garn-St. Germain Depository Institutions Act (which prohibits enforcement of due-on-sale clauses against transfers to spouses and certain relatives), but the new owner remains bound by the loan terms. Any subsequent sale or refinance must satisfy the existing mortgage.

(2) Property taxes. Past-due property taxes from the deceased's ownership remain a lien against the property and become the new owner's obligation. The new owner is also responsible for future property taxes from the date of inheritance forward. Where the property qualifies for any homestead, senior, or veteran exemption that the deceased enjoyed, the new owner must affirmatively reapply; the exemption does not automatically transfer.

(3) Recorded liens, easements, and restrictions. Any recorded encumbrance against the property — a mechanic's lien, a recorded judgment, a utility easement, a homeowners'-association restriction, a private deed restriction — continues against the property in the new owner's hands. The new owner takes subject to these encumbrances. Title insurance (see above) protects against unrecorded surprises but not against properly recorded ones.

The Income-Tax Consequences of Resolution

Real property received by inheritance carries a stepped-up tax basis, equal to the property's fair market value as of the deceased's date of death. This is one of the most favorable rules in the entire federal income-tax code. It eliminates, at the moment of inheritance, every dollar of unrealized appreciation that accrued during the deceased's ownership.

Three practical consequences follow:

1. **A sale soon after inheritance produces little or no capital gain.** The basis is the fair market value at death; the sale price is the fair market value within months thereafter; the difference is small. The new owner can typically sell without significant capital-gains tax exposure.
2. **A long-term hold produces gain measured from the basis step-up forward.** If the new owner holds the property for ten years and sells, the gain is the appreciation from the date-of-death value to the sale price — not the full appreciation from the deceased's original purchase.
3. **Documentation of the step-up matters.** The new owner should obtain a formal date-of-death appraisal — not merely the tax assessment, which frequently understates value — and retain it permanently. The appraisal becomes the documentary basis for any future sale and is the only authoritative record once decades have passed.

Appendix M treats the basis-step-up rules in detail and compares the income-tax outcomes of inheritance, lifetime gift, and joint-titling under various scenarios.

When Resolution Is Quiet

The end of post-mortem property administration is often anticlimactic. The recorded deed is filed. The title search updates. The new owner receives the documents in the mail. The mortgage company sends a letter acknowledging the new borrower. The property-tax authority sends a revised statement. None of these arrivals is dramatic. The administration ends not with a hearing or a ceremony but with a series of small administrative confirmations.

This quietness is the institution working as designed. The system is not built for ceremony. It is built for orderly transition. The orderly transition is what protects the buyers, lenders, creditors, and inheritors who will rely on the recording chain in the years to come.

> **KEY POINT**
>
> The resolution of post-mortem property ownership is a recorded event, not a felt one. The legal change is complete the moment the new instrument is recorded. The emotional change — for the family, for the new owner — runs on a separate calendar that the system does not attempt to manage.

What Resolution Permits

Once ownership is resolved, the new owner can finally do what the property was always going to permit: live in it, rent it, sell it, refinance it, gift it, divide it, or pass it on. The interim period — the months between the death and the recording — is the period in which the property is in motion, in which decisions cannot be made cleanly because authority is not yet vested. The resolution ends that period.

For many families, the practical experience of resolution is that a long-deferred decision can finally be made. The house can be sold. The vacation property can be transferred to the children's generation. The investment property can be added to a refinanced portfolio. The family farm can be put into a conservation easement. None of these were possible during the interim. All of them become possible the moment the new owner's name appears on the recorded title.

What This Looks Like in Practice

Twenty-two months after his father's death, John finally received the recorded executor's deed in the mail. The deed transferred title to the family home — a modest three-bedroom in a quiet Pennsylvania suburb — into his individual name as the sole inheriting beneficiary. The instrument bore the recorder's stamp, the book and page of recording, and the certification of the clerk.

Nothing about the day was dramatic. John was at his office; the certified mail arrived at the front desk; he signed for it and brought it back to his desk. He looked at the document for a moment, recognized what it was, and returned to his work.

Over the following two weeks, the practical changes arrived in sequence. The mortgage company, which had been corresponding with the executor, redirected its statements to John in his individual capacity. The homeowners' insurance carrier issued a new policy in his name with the same coverage limits. The county assessor sent a new tax statement with John's name where his father's had been for forty-three years.

John never told anyone in his family that the property had finally transferred. There was nothing to tell. The house had been his — economically — since his father's death. The transfer simply made the public record match what the family had already understood.

Two months later, John listed the house. The sale closed within four weeks. The buyer's title insurance issued without exception. The transfer to the buyer produced no taxable gain for John, because the basis step-up at his father's death had reset the property's basis to its date-of-death value, which was nearly identical to the sale price.

From the outside, the entire post-mortem property experience consisted of a year and a half of waiting followed by a thirty-day sale. From the inside, the year and a half had been the structural work — the creditor-claim window, the inventory, the accounting, the court approval — that made the thirty-day sale possible. The institution had done what it was built to do, in the order it was built to do it, on the calendar the law had set centuries before. The closing was quiet because everything that needed to happen had already happened.

Where We Go From Here

Notes on Practice

Two final practical notes round out the resolution discussion. First, the single most important document an heir can obtain at the moment of resolution is a formal date-of-death appraisal. The appraisal documents the basis-step-up under IRC §1014 and is the only authoritative basis figure available decades later when the property is eventually sold. The cost (typically five hundred to a thousand dollars for residential property) is trivial relative to the income-tax exposure that an undocumented basis can produce.

Second, the new owner should reapply, immediately, for every property-tax exemption that applies to their own circumstances — homestead, senior, veteran, disability. The exemptions held by the deceased do not transfer automatically. The reapplication is usually a single form, filed with the county assessor, that takes minutes and saves hundreds or thousands of dollars per year for the duration of the new owner's tenure.

The Post-Resolution Asset-Management Decisions

Once title is in the new owner's name, several asset-management decisions follow that the family is often unprepared for. The most consequential:

1. **Hold or sell.** If the new owner has no use for the property, the decision to sell is usually best made within the first year — while the date-of-death basis still produces minimal capital-gain exposure and while the property's condition is recent enough to support a favorable sale price. Holding for years and then selling can produce significant capital-gains tax exposure and often coincides with the property needing significant maintenance.
2. **Refinance or assume the existing mortgage.** Where an existing mortgage is in place, the new owner can typically continue making the existing payments indefinitely (per Garn-St. Germain protection). Refinancing into the new owner's name produces a cleaner ownership record and may improve the rate, but consumes closing costs and time. The choice depends on the rate environment and the new owner's long-term plans.
3. **Convert to rental, sell, or occupy.** Each option has distinct tax consequences. Converting to rental triggers depreciation recapture on eventual sale; selling triggers capital-gains analysis; occupying as primary residence preserves the section-121 home-sale exclusion (currently

$250,000 single / $500,000 joint) for any later sale after two years of occupancy.

4. **Insurance, security, and maintenance.** The new owner's policies must reflect actual use (occupancy versus vacancy versus rental); these categories carry different premium structures and different coverage exclusions. A policy that was appropriate for the deceased's owner-occupancy may be inadequate for the new owner's vacancy or rental use.

5. **Estate planning for the new owner.** Inheriting a substantial real-property asset often changes the new owner's own estate planning. The new owner should review their own will and trust to ensure the inherited property is appropriately addressed for their own eventual transfer. The annual review the new owner now performs on their own deeds becomes critical.

Edge Case — Continuing Trust Administration

In some estate plans, the inherited property does not pass outright to the beneficiary; it remains in trust for the beneficiary's benefit, often for life. This structure is common for surviving spouses (the deceased's children from a prior marriage are protected as remainder beneficiaries), for beneficiaries with disabilities (a special-needs trust), and for beneficiaries the deceased wished to provide for without the risk of imprudent expenditure (a spendthrift trust).

When the inherited property is held in continuing trust, the resolution is incomplete. The trustee continues to administer the property under the trust's terms; the beneficiary has the use of the property but not ownership; the remainder beneficiaries (often the deceased's children or grandchildren) wait for the current beneficiary's death or for the trust's termination event. The administration may continue for decades. The successor trustee bears the long-term fiduciary duty of preserving the property, paying its expenses from trust income or principal, and eventually distributing it as the trust directs. Counsel for the successor trustee should be familiar with both the trust agreement and the applicable trust-administration statute; the role is more complex than the comparable duty of a one-time executor.

Common Questions, Briefly

How long do I have to sell inherited property to take advantage of the basis step-up?

There is no deadline on the basis step-up itself — the basis is reset to date-of-death value regardless of when you sell. But the longer you hold, the more post-death appreciation accumulates, and that appreciation is taxable as long-term capital gain on eventual sale. Most planners recommend selling within the first year if a sale is the eventual plan, both to minimize post-death appreciation exposure and to complete the estate cleanly.

Do I have to pay capital-gains tax if I inherit property and immediately sell it?

Almost never. The basis step-up resets the basis to fair market value at date of death. Selling immediately produces a sale price approximately equal to the new basis, yielding little or no taxable gain. Selling costs (real-estate commissions, closing costs) further reduce the realized amount. Most heirs who sell within the first six months pay no federal capital-gains tax on the sale. State income-tax treatment varies; consult local counsel.

Practitioner Patterns — Beyond the Resolution

The completion of a post-mortem property transfer is the end of one process and the beginning of another. The new owner now holds property that they did not buy, did not build, and may not have planned to own. The decisions they make in the first year of ownership often determine what the property becomes — a held asset, a sold asset, a rented asset, a problematic asset. Three patterns characterize the most successful first-year ownership experiences.

The first is early decisive action. The new owner who decides — within the first ninety days — what they intend to do with the property (hold, sell, rent, occupy) almost always has a better experience than the new owner who delays the decision. Delay is expensive: the property continues to incur taxes, insurance, maintenance, and (often) utility costs without producing income or use value. Delay also tends to compound; the property that is not actively managed within the first year typically remains unmanaged for years, producing depreciation, deferred maintenance, and accumulating anxiety. Decisive action — even imperfect action — is usually better than indefinite indecision.

The second is professional engagement. The new owner who engages a real-estate professional (broker, property manager, contractor for needed repairs) within the first ninety days typically captures more value than the new owner who attempts to manage the property without professional support. Inheriting a property is not the same as having developed expertise in managing or selling it. The cost of professional engagement is real but generally modest relative to the value preserved or added. Where the new owner intends to sell, an experienced listing agent will typically generate five to ten percent more in net proceeds than a self-managed sale.

The third is the integration of the new property into the new owner's broader financial and estate plan. The inherited property is now part of the new owner's balance sheet, the new owner's tax picture, and the new owner's eventual succession. Each of these dimensions deserves explicit attention. A consultation with the new owner's accountant (for the tax implications) and estate planner (for how the property fits into the new owner's own succession) within the first six months is usually well-spent time. The new owner who integrates the property into their broader financial life retains the value efficiently. The new owner who treats the property as a separate, unintegrated asset frequently discovers, years later, that opportunities for tax efficiency and estate planning were missed.

There is no further chapter. The Conclusion follows.

Figure 10.1

The property resolution sequence — three sequential phases that complete the post-mortem transfer.

KEY POINT

The resolution of post-mortem property ownership is a recorded event, not a felt one. The legal change is complete the moment the new instrument is recorded. The emotional change — for the family, for the new owner — runs on a separate calendar that the system does not attempt to manage.

What This Chapter Has Said

Property ownership resolves when title is recorded in the new owner's name, court authority ends, and trust administration stabilizes. The three pathways — automatic transfer, trust transfer, and probate transfer — produce the same end state through different procedures. Every new owner should retain in a permanent file the recorded instrument that vested title, current title insurance, current property-tax statement, updated insurance policies, and a complete title-chain summary. Mortgages, property taxes, and recorded encumbrances continue against the property in the new owner's hands. The basis step-up under IRC §1014 eliminates every dollar of unrealized appreciation that accrued during the deceased's ownership; a date-of-death appraisal is essential documentation. The resolution is quiet by design — a series of small administrative confirmations rather than a ceremony — because the institution is built for orderly transition rather than for ritual.

CONCLUSION

What Property Law Is For

Property after death is not complicated because the law is cruel.

It is complicated because ownership is precise.

Once you understand how ownership transfers, the process becomes predictable — even if it is not always easy.

We have spent this volume on a single subject: how real property moves from one set of hands to another at the moment of death. We have examined the deeds that prescribe the transfer, the forms of co-ownership that determine what happens automatically and what does not, the trust structures that hold title across a lifetime, the three paths a house can travel after a death, the structural failures that pull houses into court, and the human disputes that arise when the transfer touches families.

What unifies all of this is the underlying logic of the recording act: a public, datable, jurisdiction-bound system of paper that allows property to outlast its owners by centuries without losing track of who owns what. The system is not designed for the family that inherits. It is designed for the orderly continuation of property law itself. The family is one of many users.

But the family is the user that matters most to the family. And it is for the family that this book exists.

This book does not tell you what to do with property.

It tells you who owns it.

If you understand the answer to that question, you are already most of the way through the post-mortem property experience. You can name what each of your family's properties will become at death. You can identify the small handful of structural failures that, in your particular case, would benefit from corrective action during life. You can anticipate the disputes that may arise after death and put the structures in place that will prevent or contain them. You can have, with the people who matter to you, the conversations that defuse most of what would otherwise become litigation.

These are not the conversations the legal system has the tools to manage. They are the conversations the family has to have for itself. The legal system can ratify what the family decides; it cannot decide it for them.

"Property law is patient. Families are not. The decisions made during life — the deeds signed, the trusts funded, the conversations had — are what determine whether the family's experience after a death is brief and orderly or long and fractured. The system rewards preparation. It does not punish its absence; it simply enforces what was already there."

Take the house seriously. Take the deeds seriously. Have the conversations the family has been postponing. Sign the documents that make the disposition match the intent. Update them when life changes. Tell the inheritors where to find the originals.

That work, done in the quiet years before the work is needed, is the highest-leverage protection any family can offer the people who will eventually inherit what it has built. Everything else in this book — the chapters on joint tenancy, on tenancy in common, on trust funding, on partition, on the tools to defuse co-tenant disputes — is in service of that single act of preparation.

Begin where you are.

— AVOY Publishing

Spring 2026

READER FAQ

Common Questions, Clear Answers

This section addresses, in brief Q-and-A form, the questions readers most commonly ask after finishing the book. The answers are intentionally short. Each one points back to the chapter or chapters where the underlying material is treated in full.

The questions are grouped into three categories. The first — Ownership & Title — covers the structural questions about how property is held. The second — Trusts & Deeds — covers the documents and instruments. The third — Disputes & Resolution — covers what happens when the family disagrees and how the matter eventually closes.

OWNERSHIP & TITLE

Q · I LIVED IN MY PARENT'S HOUSE FOR YEARS. DOESN'T THAT MEAN I OWN IT?

A · No. Occupancy and ownership are different categories. Ownership is determined by the most recently recorded valid deed, in the form of ownership that deed prescribes. Long-term occupancy with the owner's permission does not ripen into ownership; the doctrine of adverse possession requires occupancy that is hostile to the owner's interest, which a permitted family member by definition is not. See Chapter 1.

Q · MY MOM'S WILL LEFT THE HOUSE TO ME. WHY DOES THE TITLE COMPANY SAY I HAVE TO PROBATE IT?

A · Because the will does not transfer real property by itself; the probate court does, on admission of the will. Until the court orders the transfer, title remains in the deceased's name. The will is the instruction; the court is the mechanism. See Chapter 2 and Chapter 6.

Q · WHAT IS THE DIFFERENCE BETWEEN JOINT TENANCY AND TENANCY IN COMMON?

A · Joint tenancy with right of survivorship transfers automatically to the surviving co-owner at death; the will has no role. Tenancy in common does not transfer automatically; the deceased's share goes through the estate, by will or intestacy. The two forms can look almost identical on a deed and behave completely differently at death. See Chapters 3 and 4.

Q · MY PARENTS PUT ME ON THE DEED YEARS AGO. WHY IS THAT A PROBLEM?

A · Several reasons, depending on the form. If you took as a joint tenant, your share is exposed during your lifetime to your creditors, your divorce, and your bankruptcy — and the gift may have triggered gift-tax filing and Medicaid look-back consequences for your parents. If you took as a tenant in common, only the form of post-mortem transfer is affected, but you and your parents now own fractional interests rather than your parents owning the whole. See Chapter 3.

Q · DOES PUTTING A CHILD ON THE DEED AVOID PROBATE?

A · Sometimes — and at a price. If the deed creates a joint tenancy with right of survivorship, the child takes the whole property at the parent's death without probate. But the child also receives only a half basis step-up (instead of a full step-up the child would get on inheritance), the parent has made a taxable gift during life, the parent has lost some control of the property, and the child's creditors can attach the home. Most planners now advise transfer-on-death deeds or trust ownership instead. See Chapter 6 and Appendix M.

Q · WHAT IS A TRANSFER-ON-DEATH DEED?

A · A recorded deed that designates who will take the property at the owner's death — without conveying any present interest, without exposing the property to the beneficiary's creditors, and without requiring probate. The owner retains complete control during life, including the right to revoke the deed at will. Recognized in approximately twenty-eight states; check your jurisdiction. See Chapter 6 and Appendix B.

Q · I AM ON THE DEED WITH MY SIBLING. CAN I FORCE A SALE?

A · Yes. Every co-tenant has an absolute right to file for partition, and the court will order a sale (or, rarely, a physical division) even over the objection of the other co-tenants. The proceeding is slow and expensive, however, and almost always ends the family relationship. Negotiation, buyout, or a written co-tenancy agreement is preferable. See Chapter 4 and Chapter 8.

Q · WHAT IS COMMUNITY PROPERTY?

A · Property acquired by either spouse during marriage in one of the nine community-property states (AZ, CA, ID, LA, NV, NM, TX, WA, WI). It is presumed to be owned equally by both spouses; at death, half is the deceased's and half is the survivor's. Community property receives a particularly favorable income-tax basis treatment at the first death — both halves typically get a basis step-up. See Chapter 3 and Appendix M.

Q · WHAT IS TENANCY BY THE ENTIRETY?

A · A married-only variant of joint tenancy with additional creditor protections during life — neither spouse can sever unilaterally, and most TBE states protect the property from creditors of one spouse only. Recognized in approximately half the states. The tenancy converts to a tenancy in common at divorce. See Chapter 3.

Q · HOW DO I FIND OUT WHO ACTUALLY OWNS A PROPERTY?

A · Pull the most recently recorded deed from the county recorder's office (most counties offer online search). Read the form-of-ownership recital. The recorded deed names the legal owner. If the title chain is unclear or you suspect missing recordings, order a title-company search; the cost is modest and the certainty is large. See Chapter 6.

TRUSTS & DEEDS

Q · MY MOM HAD A TRUST. WHY IS THE HOUSE STILL IN PROBATE?

A · Because the deed to the house was not transferred into the trust during your mother's lifetime. The trust is a container; until property is actually retitled into it, the trust does not own the property. The mismatch between the trust agreement and the deed is the single most common failure in modern estate planning, and it produces probate of the unfunded asset. See Chapter 5.

Q · HOW DO I TELL IF MY TRUST ACTUALLY OWNS MY HOUSE?

A · Pull the deed. Read the recital. If it shows you in your individual name, the trust does not own the property. If it shows you (or any trustee) in trust capacity, with the trust's full legal name and date matching the trust document, the trust owns it. The five minutes spent on this verification, performed annually, prevents most trust-funding failures. See Chapter 5.

Q · MY REFINANCE REQUIRED ME TO TAKE THE PROPERTY OUT OF THE TRUST. WHAT NOW?

A · After the refinance closes, record a new deed putting the property back into the trust. This step is frequently forgotten, and the property remains in your individual name until death — at which point it is a probate asset, not a trust asset. The corrective deed costs a few hundred dollars and a recording fee. See Chapter 5.

Q · WHAT IS A TRUSTEE'S DEED?

A · A deed executed by a trustee in trust capacity, transferring real property out of the trust to a beneficiary or to a buyer. It is the instrument the successor trustee uses to distribute trust-owned property after the settlor's death. See Chapter 5 and Chapter 10.

Q · WHAT IS A POUR-OVER WILL?

A · A short will whose only function is to direct any asset that was not transferred into the deceased's revocable trust during life into that trust at death. It is the safety net for trust-based estate plans. The pour-over will must still be admitted to probate, but it ensures that any forgotten asset is ultimately controlled by the trust. See Chapter 5.

Q · WHAT'S THE DIFFERENCE BETWEEN A WARRANTY DEED AND A QUITCLAIM DEED?

A · A warranty deed includes covenants by the grantor that the title is good and that the grantor will defend it; it gives the grantee the strongest possible title position. A quitclaim deed conveys only whatever interest the grantor happens to have, with no covenants. Quitclaim is appropriate among family members or for trust-funding transfers; warranty is the standard for arms-length purchases. See Appendix D.

Q · WHAT IS A LADY-BIRD DEED?

A · An enhanced life-estate deed recognized in five states (TX, FL, MI, VT, WV, NM) that allows the owner to retain a life estate plus the unilateral power to convey or revoke. At death, the property passes automatically to the named remainderman, outside probate. See Chapter 6.

Q · DO I OWE GIFT TAX IF I PUT MY CHILD ON MY DEED?

A · Generally yes — adding a non-spouse to a deed is treated, for federal gift-tax purposes, as a gift of the proportional interest transferred. If the value exceeds the annual exclusion, a gift-tax return (Form 709) is required, and the gift counts against the donor's lifetime exemption. The total tax due is usually zero (because of the lifetime exemption), but the filing requirement is real. See Chapter 3.

Q · WHAT IS A DEED OF TRUST AND HOW IS IT DIFFERENT FROM A MORTGAGE?

A · Functionally, both secure a loan against real property. A mortgage creates a lien in favor of the lender, foreclosable through judicial process. A deed of trust transfers title to a third-party trustee, who holds it as security and can foreclose by non-judicial sale (faster). The terminology varies by state. The death of the property owner does not extinguish either; both continue against the inheriting owner. See Chapter 10.

DISPUTES & RESOLUTION

Q · MY SIBLING WON'T AGREE TO SELL THE INHERITED HOUSE. WHAT CAN I DO?

A · Three options. First, negotiate a buyout — you sell your share to the holdout sibling, or vice versa, at an agreed price. Second, wait — sometimes a year of patience produces a different negotiating posture. Third, file for partition — every co-tenant has an absolute right to compel a sale through court proceeding. Partition is the slowest and most expensive option but it is always available. See Chapter 8.

Q · WHAT IS A PARTITION ACTION?

A · A court proceeding to end a co-tenancy by dividing the property physically (rare for residential property) or by ordering a sale and distributing the proceeds. Any co-tenant can file. The proceeding takes eighteen to thirty-six months and consumes significant attorneys' fees from the eventual sale proceeds. The modern preference is for partition by sale at fair market value; the Uniform Partition of Heirs Property Act, where adopted, provides additional protections. See Chapter 4 and Chapter 8.

Q · MY SIBLING IS LIVING IN THE HOUSE RENT-FREE. CAN I MAKE THEM PAY?

A · Generally no, unless they have ousted you. Co-tenants in possession owe no rent to non-occupying co-tenants under the default rule. The other co-tenants' remedies are to negotiate a written occupancy agreement, demand to enter the property (refusal would be ouster, triggering rent), or petition for partition. See Chapter 8.

Q · I PAID THE PROPERTY TAXES FOR YEARS WHILE THE OTHERS DID NOTHING. CAN I GET REIMBURSED?

A · Yes. A co-tenant who pays more than their proportional share of necessary expenses (taxes, insurance, mortgage, structural repairs) has a right of contribution against the others. The right is enforceable in partition or in a separate accounting action. Document everything; the receipts are your evidence. See Chapter 8 and Table 8.1.

Q · MY DAD'S SECOND WIFE INHERITED THE HOUSE. ARE WE ENTITLED TO ANYTHING?

A · Probably not directly, unless your father's estate plan provided for you specifically. The marital home that passed to the second wife is hers; she can dispose of it however she chooses. Some states allow children of a prior marriage to assert claims under an elective-share or pretermitted-heir statute, but the typical outcome is that the second spouse takes the home and controls subsequent disposition. See Chapter 9.

Q · WHAT IS ANCILLARY PROBATE?

A · A separate probate proceeding in a state where the deceased owned real property, when that state is different from the deceased's state of residence. Real property is governed by the law of the situs, and only the courts of the situs state can direct a transfer of recorded title. Ancillary probate can be avoided by trust ownership, transfer-on-death deed, or holding the property through an LLC. See Chapter 7 and Appendix N.

Q · HOW LONG DOES IT TAKE FOR PROPERTY TO RESOLVE AFTER A DEATH?

A · It depends on the path. Automatic transfer (joint tenancy, TOD deed): two to four weeks. Trust transfer: three to twelve months. Probate transfer (uncontested): eight to twelve months. Probate transfer (contested): two to four years. See Chapter 10 and Appendix G.

Q · WHAT TAX BASIS DOES THE NEW OWNER OF INHERITED PROPERTY GET?

A · A stepped-up basis equal to the property's fair market value as of the date of the deceased's death. This is one of the most favorable rules in the federal income-tax code; it eliminates every dollar of unrealized appreciation that accrued during the deceased's ownership. Obtain a formal date-of-death appraisal and retain it permanently. See Chapter 10 and Appendix M.

Q · ARE PROPERTY-TAX EXEMPTIONS TRANSFERRED TO THE NEW OWNER?

A · No. Homestead, senior, veteran, and similar exemptions are personal to the previous owner and end at that owner's death. The new owner must affirmatively reapply for any exemption that applies to their own circumstances. The reapplication is usually a simple form filed with the county assessor. See Chapter 10.

Q · DOES INHERITING A HOUSE TRIGGER A REASSESSMENT OF PROPERTY TAXES?

A · It depends on the state. California's Proposition 19 (effective 2021) allows children to inherit a parent's primary residence with the parent's tax base only if the child uses it as a primary residence and the value does not exceed certain thresholds. Most other states do not have parent-child exclusions; reassessment to current market value is the default. The local assessor's office is authoritative. See Chapter 10.

Q · MY DECEASED PARENT'S MORTGAGE — DO I NEED TO PAY IT OFF IMMEDIATELY?

A · Generally no. Under the federal Garn-St. Germain Act, the lender cannot accelerate the loan upon transfer to certain relatives (including children) by inheritance. You inherit the property subject to the mortgage and continue making payments under the existing terms. If you wish to refinance for a better rate or to remove your siblings as co-owners, that is a separate decision you can make at your discretion. See Chapter 10.

Q · WHAT IS A QUIET-TITLE ACTION?

A · A court proceeding to resolve any cloud on or dispute about the title to real property. Used when the recording chain is broken, when adverse-possession or boundary claims are asserted, or when competing claims must be sorted out. The court's order, when entered, becomes the controlling determination of title. See Chapter 7.

GLOSSARY OF PROPERTY-AFTER-DEATH TERMS

◆

This glossary covers the principal terms used in this book, in alphabetical order. Each entry includes a brief definition and, where helpful, a cross-reference to the chapter where the term is treated in fuller context.

Adverse Possession

A doctrine permitting a long-term occupant whose use of property is open, notorious, and hostile to the record owner's interest (typically for 5–20 years, depending on state) to acquire title by judicial decree. The doctrine does not apply to permitted occupants. See Chapter 1.

Affidavit of Death of Joint Tenant

A recorded affidavit that, together with a certified death certificate, updates the public record to reflect the death of a joint tenant and the survivor's resulting sole ownership. See Chapter 6.

Ancillary Probate

A separate probate proceeding conducted in a state other than the state of the deceased's domicile, required for real property located in that other state. See Chapter 7 and Appendix N.

Basis (Cost Basis)

The amount used to determine gain or loss on the sale of property for federal income-tax purposes. The basis of inherited property is generally the fair market value as of the date of the deceased's death (the "step-up"). See Chapter 10 and Appendix M.

Beneficiary Deed

A statutory variant of the transfer-on-death deed used in some states (notably Nevada). Functionally equivalent. See Chapter 6.

Bequest

A gift of personal property under a will. Distinguished from a "devise," which is a gift of real property. Modern usage often blurs the distinction.

Chain of Title

The recorded sequence of conveyances of a particular parcel of real property, from the original sovereign grant to the present owner. The chain is the documentary basis for any current ownership claim. See Chapter 2.

Co-Tenant / Co-Tenancy

Generic terms for two or more persons who hold concurrent interests in the same real property — whether as joint tenants, tenants in common, or tenants by the entirety. See Chapters 3 and 4.

Community Property

Property acquired by either spouse during marriage in one of nine community-property states; presumed to be owned equally by both. Receives particularly favorable basis treatment at first death. See Chapter 3 and Appendix M.

Community Property With Right of Survivorship (CPWROS)

An opt-in election available in some community-property states (notably Nevada, Arizona, California, Texas, Wisconsin) that combines the basis-step-up advantage of community property with the automatic transfer feature of joint tenancy. See Chapter 6.

Contribution (Right of)

The right of a co-tenant who has paid more than their proportional share of necessary property expenses to recover the excess from the other co-tenants. See Chapter 8 and Table 8.1.

Deed

A legal instrument conveying an interest in real property from one person (grantor) to another (grantee). The recorded deed is the documentary source of current ownership. See Chapter 2.

Deed of Trust

A security instrument used in many states (in lieu of a mortgage) that transfers title to a third-party trustee as security for a loan. See Appendix D.

Devise

A gift of real property under a will. Distinguished from a "bequest" of personal property. See Chapter 2.

Encumbrance

Any recorded lien, easement, restriction, or other right burdening real property. Encumbrances run with the land and continue against successive owners. See Chapter 10.

Estate (Probate)

The set of property the deceased owned individually (or as a tenant in common) at death and that passes through the probate process. Distinguished from non-probate property (joint tenancy, trust ownership, beneficiary designations). See Chapter 6.

Executor / Executrix

The person named in a will to administer the estate, confirmed by the court through issuance of Letters Testamentary. See Chapter 6 and the companion volume Probate Explained.

Fair Market Value

The price a willing buyer would pay a willing seller in an arms-length transaction. The standard for date-of-death valuation used to set basis. See Chapter 10 and Appendix M.

Funding Gap

An asset that the settlor of a revocable trust intended to place in the trust but failed to retitle during life. The asset becomes a probate asset at death. The single most common failure in modern estate planning. See Chapter 5.

Garn-St. Germain Act

Federal statute (12 U.S.C. §1701j-3) prohibiting enforcement of due-on-sale clauses against transfers to certain relatives, including transfers by inheritance. Allows children to inherit encumbered property without immediate refinance. See Chapter 10.

Grantor / Grantee

The grantor conveys; the grantee receives. The two parties to any deed.

Heir

A person entitled by intestate succession to a share of an estate. Heirs are determined by state statute when there is no will. Distinguished from beneficiaries, who take by will or trust direction. See Chapter 4.

Heirs Property

Real property held by tenants in common as a result of inheritance, often through multiple generations without formal estate administration. Subject in some states to the Uniform Partition of Heirs Property Act. See Chapter 4 and Chapter 8.

Joint Tenancy with Right of Survivorship (JTWROS)

A form of co-ownership in which the death of one joint tenant causes the deceased's interest to vest automatically in the surviving joint tenants. See Chapter 3.

Lady-Bird Deed

An enhanced life-estate deed recognized in five states (TX, FL, MI, VT, WV, NM). Reserves a life estate plus the unilateral power to convey or revoke. Property passes automatically at death to the named remainderman. See Chapter 6.

Letters Testamentary / Letters of Administration

Court-issued documents that confirm an executor's or administrator's authority to act for the estate. Required by title companies and recording offices for any post-mortem property transfer through probate. See Chapter 6.

Life Estate

An ownership interest measured by the duration of a person's life. The life tenant has full possession and use; at the life tenant's death, the property passes to the remainderman named in the deed creating the estate. See Chapter 6.

LLC (Limited Liability Company)

A statutory entity recognized in all states that can hold real property and shield individual members from certain liabilities. Useful for multi-state real estate, investor co-ownership, and structured family ownership. See Chapter 7 and Appendix N.

Mortgage

A security instrument creating a lien against real property to secure a loan. The deceased's mortgage continues against the property in the inheriting owner's hands. See Chapter 10.

Ouster

A co-tenant's affirmative exclusion of other co-tenants from the property. Triggers a duty of the ousting co-tenant to pay the others their fair share of rental value. See Chapter 8.

Partition

A court-ordered termination of a co-tenancy, by physical division of the property (partition in kind) or by sale and distribution of proceeds (partition by sale). Available as a matter of right to any co-tenant. See Chapter 4 and Chapter 8.

Pour-Over Will

A short will whose only function is to direct any asset not previously placed in a trust into that trust at death. See Chapter 5.

Quitclaim Deed

A deed conveying whatever interest the grantor happens to have, without covenants of warranty. Common for trust-funding transfers and transfers among family members. See Appendix D.

Recording Act

The state statute that establishes the public record of deeds and other instruments affecting real property. The recording act is the foundation of American property law. See Chapter 2.

Recording (Recorded Deed)

The act of filing a deed (or other instrument) with the county recorder's office, making it part of the public record. Unrecorded deeds are valid between the parties but generally not against third-party purchasers without notice. See Chapter 2.

Remainderman

The person who takes the property at the end of a life estate or other present interest. Named in the deed creating the intermediate interest. See Chapter 6.

Revocable Living Trust

A trust created by the settlor during life, in which the settlor typically serves as trustee and beneficiary, and which the settlor can amend or revoke at any time. Becomes irrevocable at the settlor's death. See Chapter 5.

Right of First Refusal

A contractual right of one party to be offered an asset before it is sold to a third party, on the same terms. Useful in co-tenancy agreements to preserve property within the family. See Chapter 8.

Settlor (Grantor / Trustor)

The person who creates a trust by transferring property to the trustee. Synonymous with grantor and trustor. See Chapter 5.

Step-Up in Basis

The federal income-tax rule (IRC §1014) that resets the basis of property received from a deceased person to its fair market value as of the date of death, eliminating built-in gain accumulated during the deceased's ownership. See Chapter 10 and Appendix M.

Successor Trustee

The trustee who takes over administration of a trust upon the death or incapacity of the original trustee. Authority comes from the trust agreement, not from a court order. See Chapter 5.

Tenancy by the Entirety (TBE)

A married-only form of joint tenancy with additional protections: neither spouse can sever unilaterally, and (in most TBE states) the property is shielded from creditors of one spouse only. Recognized in approximately half the states. See Chapter 3.

Tenancy in Common (TIC)

A form of co-ownership in which each co-owner holds an undivided fractional interest with no right of survivorship. The default presumption in nearly every state when a deed names two or more grantees without specifying joint tenancy. See Chapter 4.

Title Insurance

An insurance policy protecting the insured against loss resulting from defects in title that existed at the time of issuance. Should be obtained at every change of ownership. See Chapter 10.

Transfer-on-Death Deed (TOD Deed)

A recorded deed that designates who will take the property at the owner's death. The owner retains complete control during life and may revoke at will. Recognized in approximately twenty-eight states. See Chapter 6.

Trustee's Deed

A deed executed by a trustee in trust capacity, conveying trust-owned property to a beneficiary or buyer. The standard instrument for distributing real property out of a trust. See Chapter 5.

Uniform Partition of Heirs Property Act (UPHPA)

A model statute, adopted in some form by approximately twenty states, providing additional protections in partition actions involving inherited tenancy-in-common property. See Chapter 4.

Warranty Deed

A deed in which the grantor covenants that title is good and promises to defend it against adverse claims. The standard instrument for arms-length sales. See Appendix D.

BIBLIOGRAPHY & REFERENCE GUIDE

◆

This bibliography lists the principal sources consulted in preparing this volume, organized by category. It is not exhaustive. It is intended as a reading map for the serious reader who wishes to investigate the underlying material in greater depth.

STATUTORY AND REGULATORY SOURCES

Uniform Probate Code, National Conference of Commissioners on Uniform State Laws, as adopted (in modified form) in approximately one-third of U.S. states. Available at the Uniform Law Commission website.

Uniform Real Property Transfer on Death Act (URPTDA), Uniform Law Commission. The model statutory framework adopted, in modified form, by approximately twenty-eight states for transfer-on-death deeds.

Uniform Partition of Heirs Property Act (UPHPA), Uniform Law Commission. Adopted in approximately twenty states for tenancy-in-common property arising by inheritance.

California Civil Code §§ 682–682.1 (forms of co-ownership), §683 (joint tenancy), and California Probate Code §§ 5600 et seq. (Revocable Transfer on Death Deed).

Florida Statutes Chapter 689 (conveyances of real property) and Florida common-law enhanced life estate (Lady-Bird) doctrine.

Texas Estates Code §§ 111.001–111.003 (joint tenancy with right of survivorship requires written agreement) and Texas Estates Code Chapter 114 (Real Property Transfer on Death Act).

New York Estates, Powers and Trusts Law (EPTL) §§ 6-2.1 et seq. (joint tenancy and tenancy by the entirety) and New York Real Property Law §§ 240 et seq.

Pennsylvania Title 20 (Decedents, Estates and Fiduciaries Code) and Title 68 (Real and Personal Property).

Illinois Joint Tenancy Act (765 ILCS 1005/) and Illinois Residential Real Property Transfer on Death Instrument Act (755 ILCS 27/).

Internal Revenue Code §§ 1014 (basis of property received from decedent), 1015 (basis of property received by gift), 2040 (joint interests), and 2056 (marital deduction).

Garn-St. Germain Depository Institutions Act of 1982, 12 U.S.C. §1701j-3 (prohibition on enforcement of due-on-sale clauses against certain transfers).

TREATISES

Powell on Real Property (Matthew Bender). The leading American treatise on real-property law. Multi-volume; covers concurrent estates, conveyances, recording, and post-mortem transfer in extensive depth.

Casner & Leach, Cases and Text on Property (Aspen Publishers). Classic academic casebook; useful for the reader who wants the doctrinal foundation.

Restatement (Third) of Property: Wills and Other Donative Transfers, American Law Institute. The current synthesis of American law on intestate succession, will substitutes, and post-mortem transfer.

Restatement (Third) of Trusts, American Law Institute. The current synthesis of American trust law, with extensive treatment of revocable living trusts.

Bogert, Bogert & Hess, The Law of Trusts and Trustees (3d ed., Thomson Reuters). The standard American treatise on trust law.

Pennell, Federal Wealth Transfer Taxation (West). Standard advanced text on federal estate, gift, and generation-skipping transfer taxes — including basis rules for inherited property.

Bittker & Lokken, Federal Taxation of Income, Estates and Gifts (Thomson Reuters). Multi-volume treatise; comprehensive treatment of basis-step-up rules.

PRACTITIONER GUIDES

American College of Trust and Estate Counsel (ACTEC) Commentaries on the Model Rules of Professional Conduct. Practitioner guidance on the ethics of estate-planning practice.

Beyer, Wills, Trusts, and Estates: Examples & Explanations (Wolters Kluwer). Plain-language overview useful for non-specialists.

Sitkoff & Dukeminier, Wills, Trusts, and Estates (Aspen Casebook Series, Wolters Kluwer). The leading academic casebook in the field.

American Bar Association, Real Property Trust and Estate Law Section, ACTEC, and state bar real-property and probate sections — practice manuals available to members.

Trust Made Simple (AVOY Publishing, 2026; Book 1) and Probate Explained (AVOY Publishing, 2026; Book 2) of The Complete Estate & Property Planning Series — the companion volumes treating, respectively, the trust as instrument and the probate process in detail. Estate Taxes Explained (Book 4) completes the four-book series.

HISTORICAL SOURCES

Pollock & Maitland, The History of English Law Before the Time of Edward I (2d ed., 1898; reissued by Cambridge University Press). Foundational treatment of the early English real-property and probate jurisdictions.

Maitland, Equity, ed. Brunyate. The classic study of the equity courts and the development of trust doctrine. Originally published 1909.

Statute of Enrolments, 27 Hen. 8, c. 16 (1535). The foundational English statute requiring public recording of real-property conveyances. Direct ancestor of modern American recording acts.

FAMILY-WEALTH AND LEGACY LITERATURE

Hughes, Family Wealth: Keeping It in the Family. The seminal work on multi-generational family wealth dynamics, including real property as multi-generational asset.

Collier, Wealth in Families. Harvard study of inherited-wealth dynamics across generations.

Daniell, Family Legacy and Leadership. Practitioner treatment of family governance and the human dimensions of legacy.

PERIODICALS

Probate & Property magazine, ABA Real Property, Trust and Estate Law Section. Bimonthly practitioner publication; particularly strong on real-property post-mortem questions.

Real Property, Trust and Estate Law Journal (American Bar Association). Quarterly scholarly journal.

Estate Planning journal (Thomson Reuters). Practitioner-oriented monthly.

Trusts & Estates magazine, monthly. Long-running industry publication.

ONLINE AND PRACTITIONER RESOURCES

ACTEC website (actec.org) and Fellows directory. The leading professional society for trust and estate practitioners.

American Land Title Association (alta.org). Industry association of title insurers and title-search companies; useful technical resources on title insurance and title examination.

Uniform Law Commission (uniformlaws.org). Source of the model statutes referenced throughout this volume.

County recorder's offices. Most counties offer online deed-search systems; the property's recorded title chain is available at modest cost. The single best source of current ownership information for any specific parcel.

ABOUT THE PUBLISHER

AVOY, LLC ("AVOY Publishing") is the publishing imprint of AVOY, LLC, a privately held company headquartered in the United States. AVOY Publishing exists to bring institutional-grade reference material on private wealth, legacy planning, family governance, and the procedural realities of American private law to readers who would otherwise rely on marketing brochures and law-review articles.

The Complete Estate & Property Planning Series is the imprint's flagship project — a four-book institutional reference that, taken together, addresses the four pillars of American post-mortem asset transfer: the trust as instrument, the probate process, the disposition of real property, and the transfer-tax regime. Each volume in the series is built to the same standard: a sophisticated subject treated with care, written for the intelligent reader rather than the specialist, structured for both first reading and long-term reference, and produced to a physical and editorial quality that respects the seriousness of the subject.

The four books in The Complete Estate & Property Planning Series:

- Book 1 — Trust Made Simple

- Book 2 — Probate Explained
- Book 3 — Property After Death (this volume)
- Book 4 — Estate Taxes Explained

Property After Death is Book 3 of the series, picking up where Probate Explained leaves off and treating, in detail, the single asset category that produces more confusion and litigation than any other in American estate practice: real property and the recorded paper that controls it. The remaining volume, Estate Taxes Explained, completes the series by treating the federal and state transfer-tax regime in the same plain-language style.

AVOY Publishing books are distributed in print (paperback and hardcover), Kindle eBook, and audiobook formats through Amazon and other retailers.

Inquiries: ap@avoyhq.com

ABOUT THE AUTHOR

◆

A. Perkins writes for people who would rather understand a thing than be told what to think about it.

A #1 Amazon bestselling author, former United States Air Force nuclear missile launch officer, holder of an MBA, and a working chief executive, he has spent his career at the intersection of high-stakes systems and ordinary human consequence. Born in Mississippi and raised in East St. Louis, Illinois, he is among the rare voices in legacy-planning literature to have navigated generational poverty, institutional pressure, and significant personal and financial trials — and to have emerged with a single, durable conviction: that everyday Americans, properly informed and properly equipped, can build extraordinary protection for the people they love.

His prior body of work — including the bestselling 21 Bars: Poetry from the Inside and Urban Poetry & Truth: The Echo of the Streets; Whispers to Mom: A Collection of Poems Celebrating Love, Resilience, and Mothers; The Intimacy Life Cycle: Fire – Fizzle – Fire; Stillness Starts Here; Beyond the Vail: An Awakening; Whispers of Love and Life — Part II; the institutional-grade reference volumes Trust Made Simple (Book 1) and Probate Explained (Book 2) of The Complete Estate &

Property Planning Series — spans poetry, mindfulness, and the lived terrain of resilience, alongside the legacy-planning subjects he has been studying for more than a decade. Across twenty-eight prior volumes — each released in both print and audiobook — and three Amazon bestseller categories, he has built a readership that returns to him for one reason above all: the willingness to tell the truth in plain language.

Property After Death is his twenty-ninth book in print, the third dedicated to the field of legacy planning, and Book 3 of The Complete Estate & Property Planning Series — following Trust Made Simple (Book 1) and Probate Explained (Book 2), and preceding Estate Taxes Explained (Book 4). It grows out of more than a decade of practical, personal experience with the administration of estates and trusts, years of close study of the property and probate codes of multiple states, and the conviction that real property — properly understood — is one of the most reliable institutions in American private law for the family that arrives at it informed. Like every prior title in his catalog, it is also available in an audiobook edition.

Mr. Perkins is the founder and chief executive of AVOY, LLC, parent of AVOY Publishing and The Complete Estate & Property Planning Series. He continues to write, teach, and speak on protection, legacy, and the long arithmetic of family wealth.

For editorial and speaking inquiries: ap@avoyhq.com

PART

◆

APPENDICES

Reference material — checklists, samples, and supplementary tools.

APPENDIX A

Property at a Glance

This appendix is a single-card reference summarizing the entire post-mortem property landscape in one place. It is intended to be torn from the book and kept with the family's working file, or reproduced electronically and shared among co-owners and successor trustees.

Table A.1

Form of ownership at death	Path	Typical timing
Sole ownership; no TOD or trust	Probate	8–12 months
Joint tenancy w/ right of survivorship	Automatic transfer	2–4 weeks
Tenancy by the entirety (married)	Automatic transfer	2–4 weeks
Community property	Probate (deceased's half)	6–12 months
Community property w/ right of survivorship	Automatic transfer	2–4 weeks
Tenancy in common	Probate (deceased's share)	8–12 months
Trust ownership (revocable, properly funded)	Trust transfer	3–12 months
Transfer-on-death deed	Automatic transfer	2–6 weeks
Lady-Bird deed	Automatic transfer	2–6 weeks
Life estate	Automatic transfer to remainderman	2–6 weeks
LLC ownership	LLC interest passes; LLC continues to own property	Per LLC operating agreement

Post-mortem property at a glance — the path each form of ownership takes.

Timing varies by state, by complexity, and by whether disputes arise. Use Table 6.1 in Chapter 6 for a more nuanced treatment of the automatic-transfer mechanisms and Appendix G for a month-by-month resolution calendar.

APPENDIX B

Survivorship Forms by State

Tables 3.1, 3.2, and 6.2 in Parts II and IV provide the principal state-by-state comparisons for joint tenancy, tenancy by the entirety, and transfer-on-death deeds. Readers preparing to work with property in a particular state may find it useful to review those tables together with the additional summary below.

Three patterns in the state-by-state survivorship landscape are worth noting:

1. **Express language is required almost everywhere.** The default presumption in nearly every state, when a deed names two or more grantees, is tenancy in common — not joint tenancy. To create a survivorship interest, the deed must expressly say so. Old deeds drafted before standard forms were computerized often did not.
2. **Tenancy by the entirety is a regional feature.** Approximately half the states recognize TBE for real property. Coverage is concentrated in the Northeast and South. Community-property states generally do not recognize TBE; they have their own marital-property doctrines that perform a similar function.

3. **Transfer-on-death deeds are gaining ground.** Approximately twenty-eight states now recognize some form of TOD deed (or equivalent). The trend over the past two decades has been toward expansion. Where the TOD deed is available, it is generally the simplest and least expensive single-property probate-avoidance tool.

The single best source of current state-specific information is the website of the relevant state's bar association, real-property section, or the recording office of the county where the property is located. The recorder's office can usually provide statutory forms and current procedural requirements free of charge.

APPENDIX C

The Heir's Property Checklist

This checklist covers the principal items an heir or successor trustee should address in the first several months after a death involving real property. It is organized roughly chronologically.

Days 1–30

- Order ten to fifteen original death certificates from the funeral home or vital-records office.
- Locate the deed to every parcel of real property the deceased owned (or believed they owned).
- Identify the legal owner of each parcel from the most recently recorded deed.
- Identify whether each parcel is in trust, in joint tenancy, in tenancy in common, or in sole ownership.
- Identify any properties in states other than the deceased's state of domicile.
- Locate any trust agreement, pour-over will, transfer-on-death deed, or beneficiary deed in the deceased's papers.
- Confirm the existence and current status of any mortgage, home-equity loan, or recorded lien.

· Notify the property-tax authority and homeowners' insurance carrier of the death.

· Maintain the property — utilities, insurance, security — pending resolution.

Days 31–90

· Engage real-property and probate counsel for each state in which the deceased owned property.

· Open any required probate proceedings (in the state of domicile and any ancillary states).

· If a trust exists and is funded, the successor trustee accepts the role and obtains a tax-identification number for the (now irrevocable) trust.

· Order a date-of-death appraisal for each parcel; retain the appraisal as the basis-step-up documentation.

· Record any required affidavits of death of joint tenant, transfer-on-death affidavits, or trustee acceptances.

· Review the deceased's homestead, senior, veteran, and similar property-tax exemptions; reapply for any exemptions to which the new owner is entitled.

· If the property is to be sold, consult a real-estate broker to evaluate market conditions and timing.

· If multiple co-owners are inheriting, schedule the family meeting to discuss occupancy, expense allocation, and long-term disposition.

Days 91–180

- Complete trust distribution or probate transfer; record the trustee's deed or executor's deed putting the property in the new owner's name.
- Obtain new title insurance in the new owner's name as of the recording date.
- Confirm the property-tax authority has updated its records to reflect the new owner.
- Confirm the insurance carrier has issued a policy in the new owner's name; address any coverage gaps.
- If multiple co-owners are inheriting, document the agreed occupancy, expense allocation, and decision-making procedure in a written co-tenancy agreement.
- Update any LLC operating agreements or trust documents to reflect new beneficial ownership.
- Retain a complete title-chain summary, including all instruments recorded post-death, in a permanent file.

An heir or successor trustee who has worked through this checklist by the end of the first six months has placed themselves in excellent position for the remaining administration. Almost every estate that resolves real property smoothly does so because the first six months were handled with discipline.

APPENDIX D

Common Deed Forms and What They Mean

Real-property practice generates a great deal of paper. This appendix names the deed forms and recorded instruments that recur most often, in plain language, so heirs and successor trustees can recognize what they are looking at when a document arrives or appears in the recording chain.

Table D.1

Document	Purpose	Who prepares
Warranty Deed	Conveys title with covenants by grantor that title is good and will be defended.	Grantor's counsel; standard for arms-length sales.
Special Warranty Deed	Conveys title with covenants only against the grantor's own acts.	Grantor's counsel; common for institutional sellers.
Quitclaim Deed	Conveys whatever interest grantor has, with no covenants.	Grantor or counsel; common for trust funding and family transfers.
Grant Deed	California-specific deed conveying with limited statutory covenants.	Grantor's counsel.
Trustee's Deed	Trustee in trust capacity conveys to beneficiary or buyer.	Successor trustee or counsel.
Executor's Deed	Executor in estate capacity conveys per court order.	Executor's counsel after court approval.
Personal Representative's Deed	Modern term for executor's or administrator's deed.	Personal representative's counsel.
Transfer-on-Death Deed	Designates beneficiary; takes effect at owner's death.	Owner or counsel; recorded during life.
Lady-Bird (Enhanced Life Estate) Deed	Owner retains life estate plus power to convey or revoke.	Owner or counsel; recorded during life.
Affidavit of Death of Joint Tenant	Together with death certificate, updates record to reflect survivor's sole ownership.	Surviving joint tenant or counsel.
Affidavit of Trust	Confirms existence of trust and trustee's authority for third-party use.	Trustee or counsel.

Document	Purpose	Who prepares
Mortgage / Deed of Trust	Security instrument creating lien against property.	Lender's counsel.
Reconveyance / Satisfaction of Mortgage	Releases the security instrument upon loan payoff.	Lender; recorded after final payment.
Easement	Grants a right to use a portion of property for a specific purpose.	Counsel for benefited or burdened party.

Common deed forms and recorded instruments — what each one does.

Each of these documents has a specific function in the recording chain. Recognizing them on receipt is most of the work of being able to track a property through its post-mortem transition.

APPENDIX E

Sample Property Letter of Instruction

A property letter of instruction is a non-binding, informal document, written by the property owner during life, that tells the eventual heir or successor trustee where the documents are, who to call, and how to find the boundary lines that the recorded instruments do not always make obvious. It is not a deed and does not modify any deed. It is the orientation document the family wishes existed at the moment of greatest confusion.

The following is a sample, adapted from common practitioner conventions. Real letters of instruction should be drafted to the family's specific circumstances and updated annually.

SAMPLE

To my family and to the executor or trustee of my estate — This letter is not part of my will or trust and does not modify either. It is offered to help you find what you will need, in the order you will need it, regarding the real property I own. Updated [date]. (1) Properties owned. I own or hold an interest in the following parcels of real property: [list each by address, county, and approximate value]. (2) Form of ownership. For each property, the recorded deed shows: [for each property — sole ownership / joint tenancy with [name] / tenancy in common with [name(s)] / trust ownership / TOD designation to [name]]. (3) Document locations. The recorded deed for each property is in [location]; copies are also held by [title company, attorney, file]. The trust agreement (if applicable) is in [location]. The most recent title-insurance policy is in [location]. (4) Mortgages and liens. The mortgage on [property] is held by [lender, loan number]; current monthly payment [amount]; payable to [address]. There are no other recorded liens against any of the properties [or list as appropriate]. (5) Insurance. Hazard insurance on [property] is with [carrier, policy number]; agent is [name, phone]. Flood insurance, where required, is with [carrier, policy number]. (6) Property tax. Property taxes for [property] are paid through [escrow / directly]; the assessor's office is [address, phone]. The current tax exemption I claim is [homestead / senior / veteran / none]; the new owner will need to reapply. (7) Co-owners and contacts. For [property held with co-owners], the other co-owners are [names and contacts]. We have / have not signed a written co-tenancy agreement; the agreement (if any) is in [location]. (8) HOA / condo association. [Property] is subject to the [association name]; current monthly assessment is [amount]; contact is [name, phone]. Restrictions and CC&Rs; are recorded at [book/page or instrument number]. (9) Practical notes. The boundary on [property] is [description]; the well is located [location]; the keys to the rental units are [location]; the password to the smart-home system is held by [trusted person]. (10) My wishes for these properties (precatory only). [Personal notes — what I hope will happen, with the understanding that the recorded instruments control]. (11) People to call first. [Trusted person 1] and [trusted person 2] know to expect this letter and will help orient you. With love and gratitude, [Signature] [Date]

A property letter of instruction is one of the highest-value, lowest-cost documents in the entire field of estate planning. It costs nothing to produce and saves the family weeks of confusion when the time comes.

APPENDIX F

Annotated Reading List for the Serious Reader

Readers who finish this volume and want to continue should consider the following sources. They are not arranged in order of importance; each addresses a different aspect of real-property law, post-mortem transfer, or the broader landscape of legacy planning.

Powell on Real Property (Matthew Bender). The leading American treatise. Verbose by intent; useful for the reader who wants the law in extended discussion.

Sitkoff & Dukeminier, Wills, Trusts, and Estates (Aspen Casebook Series). The leading academic casebook in the field. Useful for context.

Beyer, Wills, Trusts, and Estates: Examples & Explanations (Wolters Kluwer). A plain-language survey, useful as a reading companion or reference for the non-lawyer working alongside counsel.

Probate Explained (AVOY Publishing, 2026). Book 2 of The Complete Estate & Property Planning Series; treats the probate process itself in the same plain-language style. Reading the two volumes together gives the reader a complete picture of property after death.

Trust Made Simple (AVOY Publishing, 2026). Book 1 of The Complete Estate & Property Planning Series — the foundational treatment of trust structures, including the trust funding discipline that is the subject of Chapter 5 of this volume.

Hughes, Family Wealth: Keeping It in the Family. Not a real-property book, but the most influential single volume on multi-generational family wealth dynamics, into which real-property planning ultimately fits.

Center for Heirs' Property Preservation (heirsproperty.org). A nonprofit organization addressing the special problems of tenancy-in-common heirs property — its accumulation, fragmentation, and occasional loss to forced partition sales. Source of useful educational materials.

ACTEC Foundation educational materials (actecfoundation.org). Free consumer-oriented summaries of estate-planning concepts.

AARP, Estate Planning Resources (aarp.org/money/estate-planning). Free overview material aimed at the general public.

APPENDIX G

The Twelve-Month Property Resolution Calendar

This calendar is a month-by-month overview of what a typical post-mortem real-property transition looks like. Actual cases vary. Properties in automatic-transfer paths resolve much faster than this calendar shows; contested matters take much longer. The calendar shown is for an uncontested probate transfer of an ordinary residential property.

Table G.1

Month	Principal activities	Recording milestones
1	Order death certificates; locate deed; engage counsel.	Lodge will (administrative).
2	Petition prepared; appraisal ordered; preliminary inventory.	Petition filed; first hearing scheduled.
3	First hearing; Letters Testamentary issued; estate account opened.	Order for Probate; Letters Testamentary.
4	Inventory and appraisal filed; date-of-death valuation set; insurance addressed.	Inventory filed.
5	Notice to creditors published; creditor evaluation begins.	—
6	Creditor-claim window closes; claims paid or rejected.	—
7	Decision made on sale or distribution; broker engaged or distribution planned.	—
8	Property listed (if for sale) or distribution prepared; tax filings underway.	—
9	Sale closing or distribution petition filed.	Petition for distribution filed.
10	Court approval of accounting; distribution authorized.	Order for Final Distribution.
11	Trustee's deed or executor's deed recorded; new owner takes record title.	Deed to new owner recorded.

Month	Principal activities	Recording milestones
12	Title insurance updated; tax authority notified; final accounting accepted.	Order Discharging Executor.

Twelve-month property resolution calendar (typical, uncontested probate transfer).

An estate that closes real-property administration by the end of the twelfth month is a well-administered estate. Properties on automatic-transfer paths (joint tenancy, TOD, trust ownership) typically resolve in months one through three; properties on contested paths take eighteen months to four years.

APPENDIX H

The Co-Tenant Communication Framework

We have argued in Chapter 9 that the single most effective tool for preventing intra-family conflict over inherited property is regular, written communication among the co-owners. This appendix provides a framework.

The Quarterly Update

Once a quarter, on the same day each quarter, the co-owner in possession (or the designated managing co-owner) sends a brief written update to all other co-owners. The update has the same five sections each quarter:

1. **Property condition.** What the property looks like now; any maintenance issues; any work performed in the past quarter. One paragraph.
2. **Expenses paid in the past quarter.** Property tax, insurance, mortgage, repairs, utilities. Itemized list with receipts attached or available on request.
3. **Income received in the past quarter.** Any rental income, dividend income, or other revenue from the property. Itemized.

4. **Anticipated expenses for the next quarter.** Tax installments, insurance renewals, scheduled repairs, improvements. List with estimated amounts.

5. **Decisions or discussions for the co-owners.** Any matter requiring co-owner consent or input — proposed improvements, lease renewals, discussions of sale or buyout. Plain language.

The update should be no longer than two pages plus attachments. It should be sent to all co-owners simultaneously, with each as a named recipient — not as a forwarded message. The same update should not vary between co-owners. Consistency is the entire point.

When a Major Decision Must Be Made

When a decision must be made that requires co-owner consent — sale, refinance, major capital improvement, lease to a third party — the cleanest approach is:

1. **Provide written notice of the proposed decision to all co-owners at the same time.** Include the relevant terms, the timing, and the alternatives considered. No surprise.

2. **Set a reasonable response window.** Two to four weeks for most decisions; longer for major matters. State the deadline clearly.

3. **Hold a structured meeting (in person, by phone, or by video) to discuss.** Allow each co-owner to express their

position. Take notes. Distribute the notes after the meeting.

4. **Document the decision in writing, signed by all consenting co-owners.** If unanimity is not reached, document each position. Some decisions require unanimity; some can proceed by majority; the co-tenancy agreement (if any) controls.

5. **Implement the decision according to its terms.** Once documented, follow the decision precisely. Most post-implementation disputes are about deviations from what was agreed.

Co-owners who follow this framework rarely end up in partition court. Co-owners who do not follow it — who let decisions accumulate informally, who allow expenses to mount without documentation, who deal with one branch of the family but not another — discover that the legal default rules favor whoever is willing to file a petition first.

APPENDIX I

Subject Index

The following index lists principal terms and concepts treated in this volume, alphabetically, with the chapter (and where useful, the table or figure) where each is treated. Page-precise references are available in the printed edition.

APPENDIX J

A Reader's Quick-Start Guide

If you have come to this book because someone has just died and there is real property to deal with, this appendix is a single-page distillation of the most important early steps. It is not a substitute for the full chapters, but it will get you oriented in the first week.

What to Do First

1. **Order ten to fifteen original death certificates.** From the funeral home or the vital-records office.
2. **Find every deed.** For every parcel of real property the deceased owned. The title company can produce them; the county recorder's office is the alternative source.
3. **Read the form-of-ownership recital on each deed.** Sole ownership; joint tenancy; tenancy in common; tenancy by the entirety; trust ownership. This determines the path each property travels.
4. **Secure each property.** Locks. Mail. Utilities. Pets. Insurance verification. Address security alarms and password access.

5. **Engage real-property and probate counsel.** One attorney per state in which the deceased owned property. The first meeting is often at low or no cost.

What Will Take Time

- Properties on automatic-transfer paths (joint tenancy, TOD, trust): two to twelve weeks.
- Probate transfers in the state of domicile: typically eight to twelve months.
- Ancillary probate in a foreign state: an additional six to twelve months.
- Contested matters (will contests, partition, quiet-title): twelve to forty-eight months.
- Final basis-step-up documentation: complete by month two; useful for years.

What to Avoid

- Distributing personal property from inside the house before authority is in hand.
- Selling or refinancing before the deed is in the new owner's name.
- Letting any insurance lapse during the transition window.
- Negotiating co-tenant arrangements without writing them down.

- Acting on advice from family members who have heard probate horror stories.

What to Read in This Book First

Chapter 6 (the three paths a house can travel), Chapter 10 (how ownership resolves), Appendix C (the heir's property checklist), and Appendix G (the twelve-month resolution calendar). Those four sections together cover roughly ninety percent of what you need to know in your first week.

APPENDIX K

Notes on The Complete Estate & Property Planning Series

The Complete Estate & Property Planning Series is AVOY Publishing's flagship project — a four-book institutional reference that treats, taken together, the four pillars of American post-mortem asset transfer. The series is written for the intelligent reader who is tired of being talked down to. Each volume is designed to be read on its own. The four volumes also cross-reference one another for readers who wish to build a broader picture.

The Four Books in the Series

The series is organized around the four mechanisms by which American families transfer wealth at and after death — and the four matters every family should understand before the transfer occurs.

1. **Book 1 — Trust Made Simple.** The foundational treatment of the trust as instrument: revocable and irrevocable, intra-vivos and testamentary, with extended treatment of the trust-funding discipline that determines whether a plan actually works at death.

2. **Book 2 — Probate Explained.** The institutional-grade explanation of probate itself: what it is, when it happens, who runs it, why it takes the time it takes, where families get stuck, and how it ends. The starting point for any reader who has just lost someone or is preparing for what comes.

3. **Book 3 — Property After Death (this volume).** The volume you are reading. Real property — houses, land, vacation homes, farms, fractional interests — is the asset Americans most often own, most often misunderstand, and most often litigate. This book treats how property moves at and after death in the same plain-language style as the rest of the series.

4. **Book 4 — Estate Taxes Explained.** The capstone volume — the federal and state transfer-tax regime explained for the family that has the assets to be exposed to it but no specialist on retainer. Estate tax, gift tax, generation-skipping transfer tax, basis step-up rules, and the planning architecture that minimizes the tax and preserves the wealth.

Reading the Series Together

The four volumes share a deliberate architecture. Trust Made Simple establishes the principal probate-avoidance vehicle. Probate Explained treats the alternative — the court-supervised transfer that occurs when no trust applies. Property After Death drills into the asset category that produces the most family pain regardless of which path applies. Estate Taxes Explained treats the tax overlay that shapes the entire structure for substantial estates.

Read in order, the series gives you a complete mental model of post-mortem asset transfer in American private law. Read individually — each volume stands alone — and you will still have a definitive treatment of the subject the title names.

Future Editions and Notification

AVOY Publishing intends to maintain each volume in the series with periodic editions reflecting changes in tax law, state statutes, and practice. Readers who would like to receive notice of future editions, supplementary materials, or additional volumes can request to be added to the series notification list at ap@avoyhq.com.

APPENDIX L

Chapter-by-Chapter Summary

This summary is intended for readers who have completed the book and want a single page that captures the principal idea of each chapter. It is also useful for readers returning to the book years later and looking for a particular treatment without re-reading the full text.

Chapter 1 — Ownership Is Not the Same as Occupancy

Real-property ownership is determined by the recorded deed, in the form of co-ownership the deed prescribes. Occupancy, financial contribution, and family expectation are not factors the recording act considers. Three common misconceptions — constructive ownership through possession, moral ownership through caregiving, and survivorship through cohabitation — produce most of the surprise post-mortem outcomes.

Chapter 2 — Why Deeds Matter More Than Wills

A deed transfers property; a will expresses intent. For property whose deed prescribes its own transfer (joint tenancy, TOD, trust), the will is irrelevant. The deed controls first; the will controls only what the deed has left to it. Two people with identical wills can produce sharply different outcomes because their deeds were not the same.

Chapter 3 — Joint Tenancy and the Myth of "It Just Goes to Them"

Joint tenancy with right of survivorship transfers automatically at death without probate, but the price is the loss of testamentary control, lifetime exposure to co-tenant creditors, partial basis-step-up loss, gift-tax filing obligations, and unilateral severance risk. Often the right form for first marriages; often the wrong form for blended families and adult-child planning.

Chapter 4 — Tenants in Common: When Ownership Splits Instead of Transfers

Tenancy in common is the default form of co-ownership in nearly every state. Co-owners hold fractional interests with no survivorship; the deceased's share passes through the estate. Common origins are inheritance, co-investment, default at conveyance, and conversion from joint tenancy. Partition is the absolute remedy of last resort and is always available.

Chapter 5 — Trust-Owned Property

A trust holds title only when property is actually retitled into it. The funding gap — assets the settlor intended but failed to retitle — is the single most common failure in modern estate planning. Trust ownership avoids probate, preserves privacy, and produces the same basis step-up at death as individual ownership. The successor trustee's authority comes from the trust agreement, not from a court order.

Chapter 6 — What Happens to the House at Death

Real property travels one of three paths after death: automatic transfer (joint tenancy, TOD, life estate), trust transfer (trust ownership), or probate transfer (sole ownership or tenancy in common). The path is determined entirely by the form of ownership at the moment of death and cannot be changed retroactively.

Chapter 7 — Why Some Houses Get Pulled Into Court

Six recurring patterns — improper titling, outdated deeds, incomplete trust funding, conflicting ownership claims, multi-state property, and tort or specific-performance claims — account for the great majority of post-mortem real-property court proceedings. Each is anticipatable; most are preventable with annual review of the deeds.

Chapter 8 — Common Property Disputes After Death

Co-tenant disputes typically revolve around four questions: who can live there, who pays expenses, who decides whether to sell, and who controls access. The legal rules — possession, contribution, ouster, partition — are settled but rarely match the family's expectations. The cure for most disputes is a written co-tenancy agreement entered into before the conflict appears.

Chapter 9 — Why Families Fight Over Houses

Houses represent stability, memory, and perceived fairness. Five recurring conflict patterns — the unequal inheritor, the blended-family second-marriage outcome, the sibling who lived there, investor co-owners turned sentimental co-owners, and the property nobody wants — produce most of the post-mortem disputes. The legal system can resolve the technical questions; only the family can resolve the emotional ones.

Chapter 10 — How Property Ownership Finally Resolves

Ownership resolves when title is recorded in the new owner's name, court authority ends, and trust administration stabilizes. The new owner should retain a permanent file of the recorded instrument, current title insurance, the date-of-death appraisal, and updated property-tax and insurance documentation. Resolution is quiet by design; it is the institution working as it was built to work.

APPENDIX M

Basis Step-Up Tables — How Inherited Property Is Taxed

One of the most consequential federal income-tax rules in American private law is the basis-step-up provided by Internal Revenue Code §1014. Property received from a decedent receives a basis equal to the property's fair market value as of the date of the decedent's death. The unrealized appreciation that accrued during the decedent's lifetime is, in effect, forgiven for income-tax purposes.

This appendix presents the basis treatment of real property across the principal scenarios — inheritance, lifetime gift, joint titling, community-property treatment — and identifies the planning consequences.

The Basic Rule

Under IRC §1014, inherited property's basis is reset to the fair market value as of the decedent's date of death (or, at the executor's election, the alternate valuation date six months later, where applicable). The pre-death basis is discarded. The accumulated appreciation, no matter how large, produces no income-tax consequence to anyone.

Lifetime gifts work differently. Under IRC §1015, the donee of a gift takes the donor's original basis (the carryover basis), with limited exceptions. The accumulated appreciation follows the property and produces a capital-gains tax for the donee on eventual sale.

Comparing the Outcomes

Table M.1

Transfer mechanism	Basis to recipient	Income-tax consequence
Inherited from decedent (sole owner)	Fair market value at date of death	Pre-death appreciation forgiven.
Inherited from decedent (trust ownership)	Fair market value at date of death	Same — IRC §1014 applies; revocable trust does not change result.
Surviving joint tenant (non-spouse)	Half stepped up; survivor's half retains carryover basis	Half of pre-death appreciation forgiven.
Surviving joint tenant (spouse, non-CP state)	Half stepped up; survivor's half retains original basis	Half of pre-death appreciation forgiven.
Surviving spouse (community property)	Both halves stepped up to FMV at first death	All pre-death appreciation forgiven.
Surviving spouse (CPWROS election)	Both halves stepped up; automatic transfer at death	All pre-death appreciation forgiven.
Lifetime gift to child	Carryover (donor's original basis)	Pre-gift appreciation taxed to donee on later sale.
Quitclaim into revocable trust during life	No change (settlor still treated as owner)	No income-tax effect.
Sale to family member at fair market value	Buyer's purchase price	Pre-sale appreciation taxed to seller.

Basis treatment of real property under various transfer scenarios.

Why the Basis Step-Up Favors Inheritance Over Lifetime Gift

Consider a parent who owns a home with original basis of $80,000 and current fair market value of $720,000 — a not-atypical scenario for a long-term homeowner in any major American metropolitan area. The unrealized appreciation is $640,000.

If the parent gifts the home to an adult child during life, the child takes a basis of $80,000 (the parent's carryover basis). When the child later sells for $720,000, the child recognizes $640,000 of long-term capital gain — producing federal capital-gains tax of approximately $96,000 to $152,000 (depending on the child's tax bracket and state of residence).

If the parent instead retains the home until death and the child inherits at the parent's death, the child takes a basis of $720,000 (the date-of-death fair market value). When the child sells for $720,000, the child recognizes no gain. The $640,000 of pre-death appreciation is forgiven.

The income-tax savings of inheritance over lifetime gift, in this scenario, exceeds $96,000. For larger or longer-held properties, the savings can be much larger. This is the principal reason estate planners discourage lifetime gifting of appreciated real property and recommend trust ownership or transfer-on-death deeds (which produce inheritance treatment) instead.

The Community-Property Advantage

The single most favorable basis treatment under American tax law is the double basis step-up available to surviving spouses in community-property states. Under IRC §1014(b)(6), both the deceased spouse's half AND the surviving spouse's half of community property are treated as receiving a basis step-up at the first spouse's death.

This is dramatically more favorable than the half step-up produced by joint tenancy in non-community-property states, in which only the deceased's half is stepped up. Spouses moving from a community-property state to a non-community-property state should consult counsel before retitling marital real estate in joint tenancy with right of survivorship — joint titling can inadvertently sacrifice the double basis step-up that the original community-property treatment would have preserved.

The Date-of-Death Appraisal

Figure M.1

Sample case: home with $80,000 basis, $720,000 fair market value

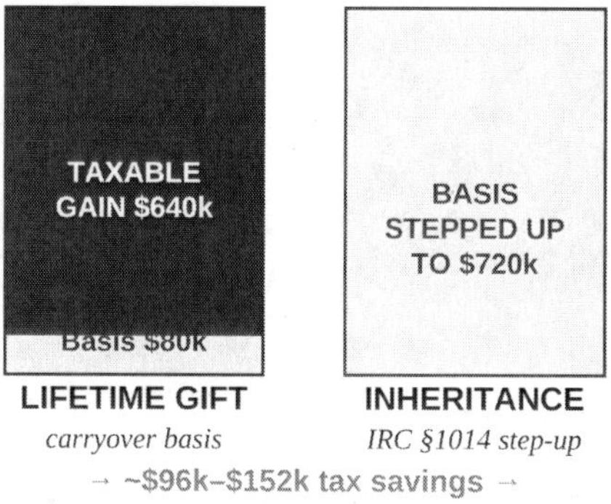

Lifetime gift vs. inheritance — the basis step-up at death eliminates pre-death appreciation from the income-tax base.

The basis-step-up is documented by an appraisal of the property's fair market value as of the date of the decedent's death. The appraisal should be obtained promptly — within the first ninety days, ideally — for two reasons. First, contemporaneous appraisals are much more defensible to the IRS than appraisals reconstructed years later. Second, the appraisal becomes the documentary basis for any future sale, and the only authoritative record once decades have passed.

The cost of a residential appraisal is typically five hundred to a thousand dollars. The cost of an undocumented basis can easily run into the tens of thousands of dollars when the property is eventually sold. The economics of obtaining the appraisal are unambiguous.

APPENDIX N

Ancillary Probate and Multi-State Real Property

Ancillary probate is the proceeding required when a deceased person owned real property in a state other than their state of domicile. This appendix explains what triggers ancillary probate, how it works, and how to manage the additional administrative burden it produces.

What Triggers Ancillary Probate

Real property is governed by the law of the state in which it is located, regardless of where the owner lived. When a Florida resident dies owning a vacation home in North Carolina, the Florida probate (the principal probate) administers everything except that vacation home. North Carolina law — specifically, North Carolina probate procedure — administers the vacation home in a separate ancillary proceeding.

The trigger is the location of real property. Personal property (brokerage accounts, bank accounts, vehicles registered in the domicile state) is governed by the law of the domicile, not by where the property is physically located. Only real property — land and the buildings on it — produces an ancillary requirement.

How Ancillary Probate Works

The principal probate proceeds normally in the deceased's home state. After Letters Testamentary issue in the home state, the executor (or local counsel retained in the ancillary state) files a separate petition in the second state, typically asking the second state's court to recognize the home-state appointment and admit the will to ancillary probate. Most states have a streamlined procedure for this — sometimes called domiciliary ancillary or foreign probate — that reduces but does not eliminate the second proceeding.

The ancillary court then issues its own Letters or its own order of appointment, which authorizes the executor to act with respect to the real property in that state. The ancillary proceeding has its own creditor-claim window, its own inventory (of the ancillary property only), and its own closing requirements. Local counsel is generally required, because the home-state executor is not authorized to practice law in the ancillary state.

How to Avoid Ancillary Probate

The cleanest way to avoid ancillary probate is to title the out-of-state real property in a way that does not require probate at all. Common approaches:

- Title the property in a revocable trust during life. The trust holds the property; no probate of any kind is required at death.
- Title the property jointly with right of survivorship between spouses (or, where appropriate, between the property owner and the eventual successor). The survivor takes by operation of law.
- Use a transfer-on-death deed (or its functional equivalent — a Lady-Bird deed in TX, FL, MI, VT, WV, NM) in states that recognize them. The recorded deed transfers the property automatically at death without a probate proceeding.
- Hold the property through a single-member LLC owned by a trust. The LLC interest is a personal-property interest governed by the domicile state's law; no ancillary probate is required.

The choice depends on the use of the property, the family's tax circumstances, and the second state's specific recognition of particular instruments. The most important moment to make this decision is when the out-of-state property is acquired, not at the eventual death — though it is rarely too late to retitle.

Estimated Time and Cost

An ancillary probate adds, on average, four to nine months to the principal administration. Cost varies, but ten to twenty thousand dollars in additional fees and costs is a typical range for an uncontested ancillary involving a single residential property. More complex cases — multiple parcels, contested title, out-of-state business interests — can add substantially to both the calendar and the cost.

The economics of avoiding ancillary probate, in other words, almost always favor the planning. A two-thousand-dollar deed filing during life saves a fifteen-thousand-dollar proceeding after death.

What to Do This Week If You Own Out-of-State Property

1. **Inventory every parcel of real property you own, by state.** Include vacation homes, inherited property, investment real estate, time-shares, and any fractional interests.

2. **Identify the form of ownership for each.** Pull the deed; read the recital. Determine which path each would take at your death.

3. **Identify each parcel that is in your individual name and is in a state other than your state of domicile.** These are the ancillary-probate exposures.

4. **Address each by the most appropriate available mechanism.** Trust ownership, joint titling with a spouse, transfer-on-death deed where available, or LLC ownership. The right answer depends on the specific facts; counsel can identify the cleanest approach.

5. **Document the new structure in your estate-planning file and review annually.** Like all estate-planning structures, multi-state property structures require periodic verification to ensure they remain in place.

A FINAL WORD

On Houses, Memory, and the Quiet Years Before

◆

You have come to the end of this volume. You have read, perhaps, more about real-property law than you ever expected to need to know.

And yet what this book has been describing, in its own structured way, is something quieter and larger than real-property law itself.

It has been describing the act of taking care.

Real property exists as an institution because someone, at some point in the long history of private law, decided that the question "who owns this land?" deserved a permanent, public, and verifiable answer — an answer that did not depend on who happened to be in possession, who could shout the loudest, or who had the most powerful friends. Every recording act, every form of co-ownership, every transfer-on-death statute, every trust-funding provision is at its root the same act: the legal system reaching forward across time to protect what one person owned for the people that person eventually wanted to leave it to.

That act of structured care is what survives all of us. It survives our names. It survives the houses we lived in. It survives the deeds we signed at closings we have long since forgotten. It is the part of us that gets handed forward — not as memory, but as title.

You have learned what the deed actually says, why it controls, what each form of co-ownership produces at death, what a trust really does (and does not), how a property moves at and after death, why some properties get pulled into court, why families fight over houses, and how ownership finally resolves. What you do now with that knowledge — for yourself, for your family, for the people who will eventually inherit what you leave behind — is the real subject of this book.

Pull the deeds for every property you own. Confirm what they actually say. Retitle the ones that do not say what you intend. Fund the trust if you have one. Sign the transfer-on-death deed where it is available. Have the uncomfortable conversation with the children. Update everything once a year. Tell the eventual successor trustee where the originals live.

Live the rest of your life with the quiet knowledge that the structure is in place.

"A plan is not made in the moment of crisis. It is made in the quiet years before the crisis, and tested — silently, invisibly —

every day thereafter. The legacy worth leaving is the one your loved ones never have to wonder about."

And so the book ends where it began — with a single sentence that we hope you will carry with you, and pass forward, long after you have closed these pages:

"Estate planning is not paperwork. It is the form love takes when it has to outlast the person who felt it."

Take care of yours.

— AVOY Publishing

Spring 2026

Made in United States
Cleveland, OH
06 November 2026

47625796R00182